Compact Cymru

A Social ... Llandudno

...reat Orme Miners

Angela Williams

Carreg Gwalch

First published in 2025

Publication: Gwasg Carreg Gwalch

ISBN: 978-1-84524-638-9
Cover design: Eleri Owen

Published by Gwasg Carreg Gwalch,
12 Iard yr Orsaf, Llanrwst, Wales LL26 0EH
tel: 01492 642031
email: books@carreg-gwalch.cymru
website: www.carreg-gwalch.cymru

Contents

Introduction

To quote Arthur R. Hughes in the souvenir book of the 1939 Llandudno Conference; '*the mines and miners belong to the past, but it was the miners who migrated to the Great Orme in the latter part of the eighteenth century and the early years of the nineteenth who laid the foundation stones for modern Llandudno*'[1]. In this book I intend to tell the stories of just a few of these miners and their families, how their lives and connection to the mines are intertwined with the growth of the town from a small mining community to the establishment of what would ultimately become known as The Queen of Welsh Resorts.

A lot of the individuals included in this book were directly employed at the mines, though some were connected to the copper industry more tangentially, but in many ways Llandudno's story can be traced back to Old Mine, New Mine and Tŷ Gwyn Mine and the people that kept the wheels of industrial activity turning. In the nineteenth century Llandudno underwent a huge change, from being a small mining village where Welsh was the predominant language, to a town purpose built for the leisure of thousands of visitors per year.

I have pieced together the lives of those included in this book by use of a mixture of historical records, history books, as well as newspaper accounts from the time, and have sometimes been privileged enough to speak with miners' direct descendants and wider family, with the view that the patchy accounts of the miners' lives that exist today can be consolidated in the hope of preserving their stories for years to come. Where possible I have tried to include firsthand accounts from the time, to be able to hear the words of the people that met some of the subjects of this book. During my research I found for some individuals the historical records were plentiful, for others their stories exist today in only the censuses and parish records, but I felt it important that, however little detail there may be, these men and women needed their place in Llandudno's history recorded.

---

1 Arthur Hughes '*Llandudno Conference 1939*'.

The abandoned Old Mine circa 1900, and beyond, some of the homes and places of worship of the community had grown around it.

I began writing this book with the purpose of forming an anthology of brief biographies and summarisations of the lives of some of the miners and their families, highlighting the significant role each played. As there were hundreds of Llandudno miners, inevitably I've been unable to include all of them in this book, and for that reason further research and study will continue.

Today in the town the legacy of the miners is living on and thriving in the miners' descendants that reside locally and contribute to the continued growth and preservation of this beautiful area, and in what the mining community created beyond the mines themselves, and in doing so, gifted to us.

Between these pages you will find lives categorised into various chapters, though this was no easy task, as one life cannot be so easily pigeonholed, however I believe each individual has been placed in the chapter most befitting to how they are remembered today.

It has been a privilege to research and write of the lives of every single one of these people and discover the rich tapestry that is Llandudno's eighteenth and nineteenth century social history.

Chroniclers and Collectors

This book would not have been possible without the works of those in this chapter, who preserved the history and stories of the characters of Old Llandudno, more than a century before my research began.

Thomas Kendrick
Image: Thomas Kendrick Library

Thomas Kendrick

Thomas Kendrick's story is one of '*rags to riches*'[2]. He rode the wheel of fortune which took him from a life of anonymous obscurity in amongst many like him who were suffering nineteenth century poverty, to fame for his archaeological discoveries.

He was born Thomas Cynric in Llandudno in November of 1821 and amongst his siblings he was the eldest of four. In the following years the family changed their surname to 'Kendrick'. His father William worked at the Llandudno Copper Mines, so in Thomas' early years his family would have had a regular and steady income. Sadly though this was not to continue, William Kendrick died in 1834, which left the family in poverty, and so Thomas, his mother and siblings went to

---

2 Dr. Cleanth Jones '*Thomas Kendrick Llandudno's Cave Man*'

live in Ysceifiog to receive poor law relief.

By the time of the 1851 census Thomas and his brother William are listed as living in Llandudno and working as copper miners, affording the family that steady income again. However, Thomas' fortunes continued to rise. When the 1871 census was taken Thomas was no longer a copper miner, but had become a 'Lapidary'. It was during this time that Thomas would make one of the most significant archaeological discoveries in Wales and this discovery would draw '*many hundreds*'[3] to his workshop on Great Orme. Thomas had discovered in a cave on his property, several human and animal bones including the famous decorated horse jaw that was eventually dated to be from the Upper Palaeolithic era, a staggering 13,500 years old!

Observing the obvious enthusiasm for his discoveries, from both scientists and tourists alike, Thomas established at his workshop what would later be described as a '*magnificent museum*'[4] where he displayed his archaeological finds. At this museum he also sold to visitors stones he had discovered on the beach and then decoratively polished. This format resembles quite the modern heritage attraction with souvenir giftshop, perhaps able to lay claim to being Llandudno's first museum!

Kendrick's Cave came to be known throughout the archaeological community and Professor William Boyd Dawkins identified Thomas' discoveries. Quite rightly Dr. Cleanth Jones in his book '*Thomas Kendrick Llandudno's Cave Man*' asserts that although it took prominent academics such as Boyd Dawkins to put the finds on the map, it was Kendrick who had '*immediately recognised that the finds were significant*'.[5]

Charging people to visit his workshop and walk his gardens Thomas was able to save a quantity of money, that he further invested into the tourist side of the town when he purchased the Camera Obscura (near Happy Valley) and charged 2d per person to enter. Close to the Camera Obscura Thomas would make yet another archaeological discovery, this time of Roman Coins.

3 *Llandudno Advertiser and List of Visitors* – 30th December 1897
4 *Carnarvon and Denbigh Herald and North and South Wales Independent* – 31st December 1897
5 Dr. Cleanth Jones '*Thomas Kendrick Llandudno's Cave Man*'

He died in 1897 of '*heart failure and bronchopneumonia*'[6], leaving a will of £436 (close to £50,000 in value today). Because of his life and the excavations he carried out, not only was a lot discovered about prehistoric Llandudno that might have otherwise remained unknown, but the archaeological knowledge of Britain was further enriched. Thomas was buried in St Tudno's Churchyard on Great Orme.

It was Thomas' ambition to own the most superior collection of historical artefacts in the country, and I believe he certainly realised that ambition! Today part of what is now appropriately named The Kendrick Collection is held in the British Museum and some more locally in Llandudno Museum. This collection has demonstrated that Llandudno had inhabitants far earlier than the Bronze Age, and who knows what more might be learned from these finds in the future.

Llandudno chronicler and miner Thomas Rowlands, looking very learned as he pours over some papers, perhaps reading his work Yr Hen Landudno. With thanks to Conwy Archive, CCBC.

Thomas Rowlands

Undoubtedly a large amount of the content of this book would not have been possible without the work of Thomas Rowlands, he is the definitive nineteenth century Llandudno Chronicler and whose work a lot of my research is steeped in. Rowlands ensured that stories and events

6 Dr. Cleanth Jones '*Thomas Kendrick Llandudno's Cave Man*'

were preserved by carefully describing the village he once knew and the characters that inhabited it. Because he articulated it with such colour, we can visualise the people and almost tangibly touch the sights. For piecing social history together records and newspapers make for excellent research material, but Thomas' work so beautifully preserved the character of Llandudno in the nineteenth century, that from '*Yr Hen Landudno*' (later translated into English by Llandudno historian Tom Parry) one gets to walk with Thomas through the town that he knew simply by reading the script on the page. No amount of research of parish records or newspaper articles can substitute for that. For this we are extremely fortunate that Thomas Rowlands put pen to paper and that he was '*a writer of no mean ability*'[7].

Thomas was born in 1835 in a house in Castle Street, in the historic town of Conwy, moving to Llandudno as a small child upon the death of his father. Like many other children living in the mining village at that time, at the age of nine he began working, picking copper ore from the stone that had been extracted from the Orme, to prepare it for shipping and smelting. This task earned him the wage of 4 pence per day working close to where the West Shore boating pond is now located.

Eventually as he moved from childhood to adulthood he found employment as a miner working under Captain Trevethick. This career would take him beyond Llandudno, to Penmaenmawr and Betws-y-coed to work in the quarries in those areas, before he ventured to Liverpool to work at the gas works. At the time of his return to Llandudno the town was in need of a new water supply. Llandudno had grown beyond the capacity that the springs of Great Orme could support and so Thomas Rowlands joined with two other men to seek another water source. After roving the surrounding area, Thomas suggested that Llyn Dulyn become that new source and after consideration the men agreed. Thus Llyn Dulyn provided the drinking water for Llandudno for many decades after.

A man of strong religious faith, his father having been a minister in Henryd,

7 *Llandudno Advertiser and List of Visitors* – 2nd January 1903

Thomas eventually became a deacon and preacher and by the time of the 1871 census he had married and started a family. However in 1872 his life was struck by personal sorrow. He and his wife Elizabeth lost their son, Thomas Gilder Rowlands not long before his fourth birthday and fate would once more be cruel to them in the same way, when they lost yet another child, Harry Ernest Rowlands on July 4th 1879 aged just twenty months old.

Thomas Rowlands died on 23rd December 1902 from '*an affection of the heart*'[8] and was buried in St Tudno's Churchyard, reunited in the ground with his two sons lost so devastatingly early. His work has been translated into English from his native Welsh, and published in local newspapers, as well as forming great research for history books by providing a window into a period of time, though now gone, through his writing it can be viewed from the modern day. It is very clear from Thomas' work that he had a lot of love for the people of Llandudno and enormous care for the town, on recalling the past he stated '*there lived here then some notable characters...honest and true as steel*'[9].

John Williams

It is said that the goddess Fortuna sits spinning the wheel of fortune, we rise up on it, and we fall, seemingly at random. John Williams is perhaps an example of the wheel of fortune playing out during one man's life, providing thrills and adventures along the way. A lot of his story is so well preserved as in 1911 he gave an account of his life to G.A. Humphreys of the Llandudno Field Club. This account includes invaluable detail about the mines and mining life in the nineteenth century.

Born in Llanelian in 1836 when he was twelve he moved to Llandudno to work in the mines. Working his teenage years in the Llandudno copper mines he left for America as a young man. After sixteen years of '*hunting bears, moose and gold*'[10] (Draper *Paupers, Bastards and Lunatics*) John returned to a very different Llandudno. The Llandudno he returned to was an established bathing resort, many of those he had known to be miners had now

8 *Llandudno Advertiser and List of Visitors* – 2nd January 1903
9 Thomas Rowlands '*Memories of Llandudno*'
10 Christopher Draper '*Paupers, Bastards and Lunatics*'

2 Cromlech Road, the house where John Williams lived for several decades after returning to Llandudno from the USA. Image with thanks to Rebecca Devany.

turned their hands to other occupations and Tŷ Gwyn Mine had long since ceased operation, with Old Mine in terminal decline.

By 1911 he was living on Cromlech Road and there he remained for the next couple of decades. However, times must have become hard for him as the years progressed along with all the difficulties old age brings with it, as by 1932 he was living in Conwy Workhouse, and died there in the infirmary that year.

John was a man that had seen Llandudno embrace tourism, which subsequently changed the town's identity as it progressed into the twentieth century. So sad then that after all his adventures John was to die in a decidedly Victorian institution, ending his life in a Dickensian fashion. Though as Christopher Draper states, mercifully John had enough money set aside to pay for his own burial, with a headstone, in St Tudno's Churchyard.

John Hughes

Another individual that provided an important record of nineteenth-century Llandudno is John Hughes whose recollections were serialised in the *Llandudno Advertiser*[11] in 1917. This account is important as it contains a lot of specific information as to the operations of the three copper mines, as well as descriptive details of the mining locations and archaeological finds therein.

John was the son of Joseph Hughes of King William, a public house located on the

11 *Llandudno Advertiser* – Saturday June 30th 1917

slopes of the Great Orme. John's involvement with the town's mining industry began when he was seven years old, employed by New Mine picking copper ore. Eventually John joined his brother Joseph at Old Mine, both were hired to clear a spoil heap that was known as Lawr Fawr. The removing of this spoil would take the pair eighteen months. It may have been during this time that John and Joseph realised that together they had a good working partnership, as mentioned in chapter *The Heart of the Community*, the pair would eventually move from mining into their father's trade, establishing a building business and coal merchants. This business would construct '*the greater part of one side of Church Walks, almost the whole of South Parade, several houses in North Parade and about a dozen shops on Mostyn Street*' (*Llandudno Advertiser*) as well as a lot of Craig-y-Don. Along with his brother, John literally sculpted Victorian Llandudno. '*It would merely be an unnecessary accumulation of words to attempt to record all that has been achieved by them to bring Llandudno to its present high standard. The buildings constructed by them speak far more eloquently than words can describe*' (*Rowlands*[12]).

Since the landscape surrounding the Great Orme mines has changed so much since the mines were in operation, John's serialised recollections have preserved detail that modern archaeologists and historians are able to draw on today. Sights that John saw, such as '*hanging from the roof big stalactites like branches of trees*'[13] in the mine's famous (now lost) cavern that was discovered in 1849, as well as a seven foot deep well that he supposed had been used by the ancient miners for washing copper ore. The well was filled with slime and John's father would go onto sell this copper rich slime for a decent profit.

Records show that throughout his life John had a very successful career, and in his eighties remained a businessman, as a respected estate agent within the town. Not just a man of business though, during his life he had also had a family, children and a wife, Marianne.

Recollections of *Old Llandudno* was so popular with the readership of the *Llandudno Advertiser* that letters were

12 Thomas Rowlands – *Adgofion am Landudno*

13 *Llandudno Advertiser* – Saturday June 30th 1917

received from the public by the publication requesting more detail on the mines and the location of the old mining shafts, which John duly provided, and ultimately this would become a wonderful first-hand account of Llandudno as it was.

Heroes and Heroism

Samuel Edwards

Born in 1821 Samuel was the son of John and Sarah Edwards. A copper miner most of his life he was also involved in many aspects of the development and nurturing of the town in his various roles such as an Improvement Commissioner, Deacon, Sunday School teacher, member of the Odd Fellowes, Bathing Machine proprietor and a Lodging Housekeeper. On top of all that, he was evidently a very capable swimmer too, as Samuel was also a lifesaver, during his life he saved twenty people from drowning. The following is a brief summary of the events surrounding just two of those twenty rescues.

On 28th July 1862 whilst bathing in Llandudno Bay a man named Richard Jones from Eglwysbach had begun to struggle in the water. Samuel rescued Richard and for saving his life he was awarded a medal. The particulars of the rescue are vague, the medal simply says '*To Samuel Edwards of Mona View, Mostyn Street, Llandudno for having saved the life of Richard Jones of Eglwys Fach whilst bathing on the 28th July 1862*'. It need say no more, for from it Samuel's courage is evident.

On 29th July 1863, Samuel once again put the safety and welfare of others foremost. A similar story to the Richard Jones rescue, a man named Mr. G. Hyatt was swimming in the bay, but had either become tired or got out of his depth as the water began to submerge him. Quick to observe this and act accordingly, Samuel wasted no time in grabbing a lifebelt, and swam out to sea to Mr. Hyatt to give him the floatation device. That October The Royal Humane Society awarded Samuel a certificate commending his '*courageous and human exertions*' that July day.

This bravery has its impact on the modern day, for all those that Samuel saved will have descendants that would not be here but for Samuel's quick thinking and ability to not just look on from the sidelines when disaster began to occur, but involve himself and boldly intervene to result in a positive outcome.

His obituary in *The North Wales*

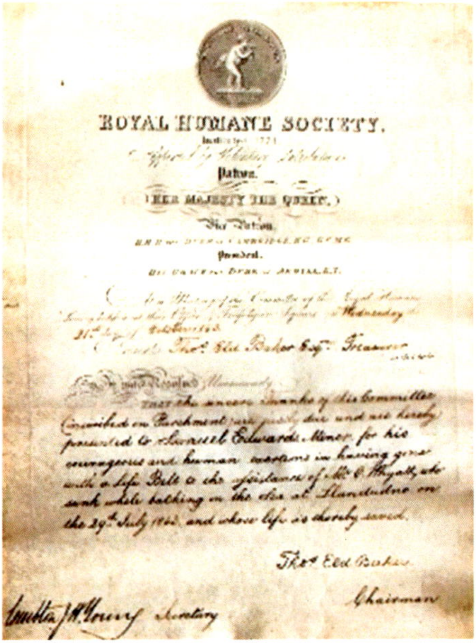

Medal and certificate used with kind permission of Samuel Edwards' direct descendant, Jason Edwards

Chronicle describes his *'jolly countenance'*[14], which must have been difficult for him to maintain at times, as during his life he had known much sorrow. In January of 1845 he lost three members of his family in quick succession, his wife, a son and a daughter all died in the space of about two weeks. This level of bereavement is difficult to imagine, even in the nineteenth century when illness and disease were never far away. How Samuel managed to move forward is a testament to his fortitude, and to the close knit community on the Morfa where he lived and who generally looked after one another. Samuel remarried and had more children, his second wife Mary

14 *North Wales Chronicle* – Saturday 16 May 1885

was the sister of Elinor the wife he had lost.

He died in May 1885, following his burial in St Tudno's Churchyard the *North Wales Chronicle* reported how highly esteemed he was, for all his many contributions to the town and what he did for its inhabitants and visitors.

Hugh Jones

Following shipwrecks such as the Rothsay Castle, the Jane Tudor and the Ocean Monarch it had become very apparent that Llandudno was in need of its own lifeboat. In the winter of 1861 Llandudno got its first lifeboat named The Sisters' Memorial in memory of a sister of two Toxteth Park women who had been regular visitors to the seaside town and donated a sum of money to establish a local lifesaving vessel. Immediately after the arrival of The Sisters' Memorial, newspapers began reporting upon the need for a capable, dependable and efficient coxswain. That man was to be Hugh Jones.

It seems very likely that a great portion of Hugh's motivation to join the RNLI may have been down to the death of his father, Joseph Jones, who had drowned during the construction of the Conwy tubular bridge (see chapter *Tragedies and Sorrows*) and his desire to prevent other families suffering the same loss. Following his appointment Hugh was coxswain of the lifeboat for more than a decade, and subsequently saved many lives. A famous rescue undertaken at this time was of the crew of the Dutch Brigantine Catharina on Thursday 4th November 1869, when Hugh and his crew went out to the brigantine

Hugh Jones circa 1870 – 1890, seated on rocks on Llandudno's North Shore. Image courtesy of Conwy Archive Service, Conwy County Borough Council.

after a North-northwest gale and a '*heavy sea*'[15] had begun to drive the vessel ashore and caused it to struggle. Although the ship was entirely wrecked, the whole crew of five were saved. For that Lady Augusta Mostyn awarded each member of the RNLI crew a half golden sovereign.

Hugh's final rescue as coxswain was on 1st January 1875. The crew went out to the Hester, a vessel that was '*exhibiting signals of distress*'[16] off the coast of Penmaenmawr. Hugh and his crew were fighting to get to the Hester for five hours, and despite the lifeboat repeatedly filling with water, the horrendous conditions and physical exertion it must have taken of the men, they did not give up but instead persevered, ultimately saving the lives of the two aboard. A formidable demonstration of strength and determination from all the RNLI crew, steered through treacherous waters by their coxswain, Hugh Jones, in their valiant efforts to preserve life.

In Hugh's role as coxswain his family were part of Hugh's lifesaving work too. If Hugh was working underground in the mine when the lifeboat was required his daughter would reportedly alert him by banging on the mine drainage pipe with a rock!

He died at his home, Rowena House on Monday 24th September 1894 and four days later he was buried in St Tudno's Churchyard on Great Orme. On the day of his funeral his fellow boatmen's homes and lifeboat house flags flew at half-mast to mark the passing and loss of someone who during the course of his career had saved many lives. His life is beautifully summarised in a newspaper of the time that stated that Hugh had '*served his generation faithfully and well*'[17].

Henry 'Harry' Davies

During the course of the nineteenth century, Llandudno saw more than its fair share of shipwrecks. In December of 1847 the Arciducapalacino (sometimes referred to as Archiduco Palatino) was wrecked in Llandudno Bay. The event clearly left an impact on Thomas Rowlands who years later described hundreds of people watching the terrifying scene of the ship as it was sinking and looking upon the

15 *Monmouthshire Beacon* – Saturday 13 November 1869
16 *Liverpool Mercury* – Tuesday 05 January 1875
17 *Caernarvon & Denbigh Herald* – Friday 05 October 1894

The serene coast off Y Fach (Happy Valley). Hard to believe when looking at such an image that is was here that it was here that the Arciducapalacino was being driven towards and the large rocky shoreline beneath.

doomed vessels crew who had '*the fear of death stamped on*'[18] their faces. Of the eleven Italian sailors aboard the brig, eight were saved and three lost their lives, those that survived owed their lives to the '*untiring efforts*'[19] (Christoper Draper) of some Llandudno inhabitants. One of those lost to the waves was the father of a boy who was also aboard the brig. Miner Henry Davies charitably took this boy into his home, and loved him as one of his own children.

Henry Davies was born in Llandudno in 1801, the son of William and Catherine Davies. In 1828 he married Mary Jones and the couple went onto have children, by the

18 ROWLANDS, Thomas – *Adgofion am Landudno*
19 DRAPER, Christopher – *Llandudno Before The Hotels*

time the 1841 census was taken they had had five children and were living on Lester Row. Most of these children would themselves become miners. Like most other families in nineteenth-century Llandudno, Henry and Mary knew the pain that was the loss of a child, their son Hugh Davies died at aged eighteen months in December of 1844, undoubtedly plunging the family into a state of immense grief and leaving a huge hole in their lives.

Perhaps this explains why when the Arciducapalacino sank both Henry and Mary were prepared to take in another child, despite not being able to converse with the Italian boy. Eventually a translator was brought to Llandudno from Liverpool. Henry obviously felt very protective of the child, who was so far from home. He refused to hand the boy into just anybody's care, none but the child's family would suffice, so that is eventually what happened, the family travelled from Italy for the handover to be done. It is difficult to determine exactly how long the boy remained with his Welsh guardian, suffice to say it must have been of considerable duration. Long enough for Henry to have formed a close bond with him and the significant amount of time it must have taken in the 1840s to get in touch with the child's family in Italy and for them to make travel arrangements and finally arrive in Llandudno to take the boy home. On the 1851 census, Henry and his family were living on the Morfa, but their temporary charge is not listed as living in their home, so it can only be assumed he had returned to Italy with his family by that time.

Henry remained a copper miner for the rest of his life and died at home on Old Road in February of 1873. The act of offering a grieving child shelter, care and sanctuary in a time before the welfare state, when everything the child needed would have to have been purchased from Henry's own finances, has earned him a place in this chapter. However, the child's life was not just saved by Henry, there were other men hard at work risking their own lives the day the Arciducapalacino sank, these men were Thomas Brookes, John Davies, John Jones, Thomas Jones, William Jones and Daniel Powell, most were miners, all were brave souls.[20]

20 *Llandudno Advertiser and List of Visitors* – 27th March 1909

The Women of the Copper Mines

The story of women in eighteenth and nineteenth century Llandudno mining is one that is mostly overlooked and forgotten. Very few records exist of women having involvement in any sort of activity connected to mining in the town, the censuses of the time not having recorded such data. However, a few written documents do exist and an oral tradition of what the women of the Llandudno mines did has been handed down in family stories. So it is out of the mirth of history that I seek to bring the stories of just three such women to the fore, the three women mentioned in mining records. In writing of these three women I hope to pay tribute to the great many that are not named in this book, such as the numerous women that dressed the copper ore to prepare it for smelting. As Owen Griffith recalled in 1897 when he reflected on the female members of the workforce of Mynydd Parys that he once knew, he said they did a '*constant task from year to year and...hard labour*'[21], washing copper ore often in cold and wet conditions. Although Griffith is speaking of another copper mine, the work would have been the same, and unfortunately for Llandudno's female population, not any easier.

Elizabeth Williams

For one of the stories of the women of the Llandudno copper mines we have to reach all the way back into the eighteenth century and to Elizabeth Williams of Ty'n y Coed Farm.

During her life she had several children, and it sounds like this life was a fulfilling and happy one, as in her will she refers to each child as being '*loving*'. Her son William was born in 1759 and she also gave birth to Evan, and three daughters, Catherine, Margaret and Jane, all five living into adulthood.

Already a widow by the time she wrote her will in 1781, on the 18th October of the following year she leased her land to William Bridge of Amlwch to mine for

21 Owen Griffith, *Mynydd Parys*, 1897 (translated by Tom Parry 2006)

The beauty of the area above Llwyn Helyg on Great Orme, part of the lands of Tyn y Coed Mine and an area that Elizabeth Williams would have been very familiar with. Now part of the Maes y Facrell Nature Reserve.

'*copper and other minerals*'[22] in the Tyn y Coed and Llwyn Helyg area of the Orme, a lease drawn up for the duration of twenty-one years and with a condition that any buildings erected for the purpose of mining should remain intact following that time. This mine was initially known as *Tyn y Coed Mine*, but in the decades that followed would come to be known as *New Mine*.

22 Porth of Aur 30658 18th October 1782

It would seem though that more or less immediately the mine ran into difficulties, despite its promising start of employing six miners, as in February of 1783 William Bridge wrote a letter stating his desire for a '*proper agent*'[23] to be appointed otherwise threatening legal action. Following this another lease was taken out by Bridge from Elizabeth for '*one peppercorn*' per year for seven years payable on the first day of St Michael (29th September). This lease had a peculiar quirk though, that if Elizabeth should pay Bridge one shilling anytime after the following April that lease would then be null and void. This new lease did little to quiet the turmoil at the site, as a Richard Ellis disputed Elizabeth leasing the land of Tyn y Coed to William Bridge. She subsequently repossessed the mines on 29th March 1783 with a notice of trespass and ejection delivered into the hands of Richard Ellis. Things were resolved by the following October and another lease between Bridge and Elizabeth was subsequently established.

Harri Gwyn Jones in his 1939 essay '*The Llandudno Copper Mines in the Eighteenth Century*'[24] suggests the leasing of the land to William Bridge at the rate of one peppercorn annually, to be a shrewd move on Elizabeth's part, meaning that under the lease Bridge would have to face any legal disagreement with Ellis instead of Elizabeth doing so herself. Although she had described herself as being '*advanced in years and a bad state of health*'[25] by the time the mine began operation, Elizabeth obviously maintained quite an astute business sense by not missing the opportunity to increase the value of her land by having a burgeoning business situated on it and knowing how to manage a legal dispute with minimal hassle for herself.

She died in January of 1785 and was buried in her hometown of Llandudno, her son William inherited the farm and the lease was maintained to William Bridge on the same terms that had been issued by his mother.

---

23 Porth of Aur – 20th February 1783

24 *Bulletin of Celtic Studies History and Law*

25 Last will and testament 1781

Elizabeth Lester

Born in 1753 she married Roger Lester and in 1782 the family lived in Amlwch, where Roger worked as a miner. By 1784, most likely drawn to the town by its growing copper mining industry, they had moved to Llandudno and ultimately resided at Tŷ Coch. They had many seemingly content and productive years together, but in 1812 Elizabeth was left a widow. Like Elizabeth Williams before her at the same mine, she entered a man's world and forged forwards in the local mining industry, holding a 10% share in the company. She was also the only shareholder to live in Llandudno and her local proximity was likely to be why she acted as the carrier for New Mine.

As well as living twenty years as a widow, during her life she lost three of her children. These children are unnamed on the headstone that they lie underneath in St Tudno's Churchyard but ultimately the whole family have been reunited, Roger and their children were all buried in the same grave, and when Elizabeth died on 1st November 1832 aged seventy-nine, she was buried alongside them.

Underneath the headstone on the far left is the final resting place of Elizabeth, her husband and three of her children.

While Elizabeth Lester was a shareholder of New Mine it rose in productivity and action, sinking numerous shafts, including one to mine for manganese at Pen-y-Ffrith. Since they were contemporaries, (Elizabeth's husband Roger having been a witness to the legal proceedings involving William

Bridge and Elizabeth Williams' son) one can only wonder if Elizabeth Lester learned from Elizabeth Williams how to navigate the male world that surrounded her.

Sarah Lloyd

A woman working in the mining industry wasn't rare in the 19th century, but Sarah is historically significant as she was a female leaseholder of a mine. However, she was less fortunate than the previous two women. Whereas Elizabeth Williams and Elizabeth Lester both benefited from being ahead of the boom in the town's copper industry, Sarah Lloyd was a leaseholder after this boom had passed.

Master Mariner David Lloyd became a leaseholder of Old Mine in 1861, and in 1864 he surrendered his current lease in order to take out a new one for the length of thirty-one years. This was ambitious as the mine was already losing money. The loss-making state of the mine was something that worried his wife Sarah, as in 1868 she wrote to the Bishop of Bangor

Pen y Buarth Farm, once adjacent to the location of New Mine, Great Orme. In the far right of the image the words 'New Milk' are painted on the farm building. Image with thanks to Conwy Archive, Conwy County Borough Council.

stating '*I try all I can to sell it but have failed to do so yet*'.[26] Interestingly, although in 1868 her husband David was still alive, this letter is evidence that Sarah already managed an amount of the administration of the mine herself, indicating her to be a woman of significant substance in a world where management roles were most definitely a man's dominion. Even during David's lifetime, it sounds as if the financial and major decision making of the mine was primarily her concern, particularly since she writes to the Bishop in the first person and not on behalf of her spouse.

After her husband's death Sarah inherited the lease of Old Mine, but this did not mean that her fortunes were made, quite the reverse in fact. Following the death of Captain David Lloyd, Old Mine continued to grow increasingly unprofitable and again she requested a number of times for it to be taken off her hands, but it was not. Instead, in the years that followed Sarah persevered, until eventually an agreement to surrender the lease was arrived at, whereby Sarah would pay £250 (a value of almost £26,000 today) to be rid of the millstone around her neck. However before the lease was surrendered she died at home at Vernon Vaults, Llandudno on 4th October 1880 leaving behind an estate of under £1,500. The surrendering of the lease, which she had for so long desired was carried out posthumously on 5th May the following year by the executors of her will[27] and so with Sarah's death Old Mine's story concluded too.

It was not just the struggles with the lack of profitability of Old Mine that Sarah faced in her life. In 1861, the same year that David took out the lease on Old Mine, the couple lost their son, John. He died off the Cape of Good Hope as he journeyed from Madras to Liverpool. The sorrow of this, compounded with the fresh responsibility of running a mine, must have made that year an exceptionally difficult one.

On Pen Morfa, Llandudno's West Shore, the only ship to have ever been built in the town, the Sarah Lloyd, was constructed. The ship was named by David Lloyd, the architect of the vessel's

26 *Great Orme Mines,* C. J. Williams 1995

27 *North Wales Chronicle* – Saturday 15 July 1882

Old Mine, the mine in which Sarah Lloyd was leaseholder, photographed in the late nineteenth century, possibly around the time that Sarah was still leaseholder.

construction, for his wife. A newspaper of the time describes the ship as being a '*well finished model, of about 70 tons burthen*'[28]. It is telling of the high regard that David had for Sarah, that he chose that the ship should bear her name. The town had great excitement and anticipation in this vessel, being the first to be built and launched in Llandudno. Many residents and visitors turned out one June morning in 1863 to witness its launch and see the Sarah Lloyd all decorated ready for the occasion. A '*beautiful, strong*'[29] vessel, and retrospectively one can appreciate how it reflects the strength and character of her namesake, through trials, and adversity.

28 *North Wales Chronicle* – Saturday 06 June 1863
29 *North Wales Chronicle* – Saturday 06 June 1863

Tragedies and Survivors

Life in the eighteenth and nineteenth centuries was often hard, for the many reasons that impacted the daily lives of those living at this time, it was commonplace to meet with adversity and devastation. In this chapter are some of the most devastating personal histories I have come across as well as tales of those that survived, even when faced with the most infinitesimal odds.

The headstone of William Brookes, St George's Churchyard.

William and Sarah 'Sally' Brookes

No mine is without its own tales of tragedy, and though the Llandudno mines suffered few fatalities in the nineteenth century, in the autumn of 1847 William Brookes, aged just thirty-three became one of those few. William was born in 1814, married Sarah Owen in 1839, and they had a family together, but he did not even get to enjoy a decade of family life before he died whilst working in the mines.

The church records simply state that he was '*killed in the minework*' and on the 2nd October 1847 he was buried in St George's Churchyard on Church Walks. His headstone is minimalist in detail, marked simply with his name and date of burial.

Following the death of her husband and the family's breadwinner, Sarah was left a miner's widow and it was now up to her to raise their children alone, and this, in a world before modern government welfare and faced with the possibility of the cold, cruel and callous realities of the workhouse, must have been a terrifying

Bathing machines at North Shore, Llandudno, c. 1880.
Image: National Media Museum Collection, WikiMedia Commons

prospect. She had lost the man she loved, and now had to summon all the strength she had to raise their children.

At this time the family lived on the Morfa, residing close to William's brother Edward. The Morfa was known to be a tight knit community and so in the absence of her husband Sarah had the love of family and friends living close by to get her through, but still she needed to source her own income. In the immediate years that followed William's death she found work as a Charwoman, earning money enough to eat and live. As the holiday resort began to develop she became a '*Bathing Woman*' owning Bathing Machines for women to use, so that they could discreetly change into swimwear and obtain some privacy as they took to the water. For the next thirty-five years until her death she attended these bathing machines on North Parade. Generations of female visitors would come to know her as 'Natty'[30], recognising her familiar, happy face year after year as they came to Llandudno on their holidays. She would dress in traditional Welsh dress, becoming an early ambassador for tourism in the town, as visitors came to know and trust her, thereby encouraging them to return to the resort. Her death in 1890 did not only leave her community saddened but the many visitors she had built a rapport with over the years.

During her fifty-two years living in Llandudno, Sarah had, despite immense personal tragedy and no doubt feeling the loss of her husband daily, developed a successful business that also ultimately benefited Llandudno's growth into a seaside resort.

Clearly a woman of determination and strength, she did not just get food on the plates of her children but raised them so that they were able to set up secure incomes and businesses for themselves, and of her sons, Owen became a chemist and William became a butcher[31].

John Smith

Only a few months after the death of William Brookes miner John Smith also lost his life at his place of employment.

In 1838 John had married Llandudno shopkeeper Anne Prichard, and chronicler Thomas Rowlands would later recall the pair's small shop, known locally as '*Siop Isaf*', as being on King William Street.

John was a deeply religious man, and became a member of the Baptist cause in 1838, and is mentioned in the Llandudno Tabernacl's *The History of the Baptists*. In this it is stated that Smith was one of the residents of the town that was in receipt of the Baptist magazine *Ystorfa y Bedyddwyr* (translates to 'The Baptist')[32]. In the years that followed John and Anne went onto have a son and a daughter, Jane and John. When the 1841 census was taken John was listed as working as an engineer

30 *Carnarvon and Denbigh Herald and North and South Wales Independent* - 17th January 1890
31 *Carnarvon and Denbigh Herald and North and South Wales Independent* - 17th January 1890
32 Tom Parry, *The History of the Llandudno Baptists.*

and the head of a young family. It seems the Smith family had everything to look forward to. However, fate would intervene and in September of 1843 John and Anne lost their daughter Jane at three years old.

Only a few years after the death of his young daughter, in May of 1848 John was killed whilst at work in the mines. The parish register marks this by simply saying 'killed in the minework'. He was buried in St George's Churchyard next to his daughter's grave. His headstone reads;

'In Memory of John Smith Shop Isaf who
Died 13th of May 1848 Aged 38 years
Having been a member of the Baptist
Church for 10 years.
Deeply lamented'.

The grave of John Smith, left, adjacent to his daughter's Jane, death separated them in life, but they lie reunited together in the ground for eternity.

Evan Davies

Evan's story is onc that stings the eyes with tears, his demise reads like something out of a novel by Charles Dickens, dying at the hand of another whilst suffering the misery that was the workhouse.

Evan was born in 1826, the son of Jane Davies who was a midwife, his father William had already died by the time Evan was christened. On the 1851 census Evan is listed as being a miner, but as the mines became less productive and his mother died he found residence with his sister and work as a labourer. Sadly, though this situation lasted for a number of years, for

Conwy Hospital, the old workhome.
(Image: Chris Draper from his book *Pampers, Bastards and Lunatics*)

unknown reasons Evan's fortunes changed and ultimately he found himself in June 1893[33] at the mercy of the workhouse.

On the evening of Tuesday 24th November 1896 Evan had a disagreement with another inmate, twenty-two-year-old Francis O'Toole. O'Toole reported that Evan had kicked him in the leg and so he had retaliated. Sadly, according to the inquest into Evan's death this was not the first time Evan had been kicked by another inmate, allegedly he had been previously assaulted by a man named Hugh Hughes[34]. Perhaps due to this, that on the night of his assault by O'Toole, Evan went to bed, dismally accepting his circumstances and abuse he received as a way of life. On the morning of Wednesday 25th November Evan was found in his bed, alive, but covered in blood. Again, not making a fuss when asked what had happened, Evan mildly replied that there was '*nothing much the matter*'.[35] He was seen by the doctor and the porter remarked that Evan was

33 *North Wales Weekly News* – Friday 11 December 1896
34 *North Wales Weekly News* – Friday 11 December 1896
35 *The Weekly News and Visitors' Chronicle for Colwyn Bay Colwyn Llandrillo Conway Deganwy and Neighbourhood* – 11th December 1896

'saturated with blood'[36]. Evan did not recover from his injuries, dying at noon on Monday 7th December. The postmortem identified a *'laceration of the neck of the bladder'*[37] and resultant subsequent inflammation as the cause of death. Francis O'Toole was found guilty of manslaughter and sentenced to one month's imprisonment[38].

Evan's deposition was read at the inquest, where heartbreakingly he seems to hold no anger towards his assailant, and instead defends him. To close I shall let Evan be heard in his own words: *'On the 24th of November I was coming through the men's yard, and the prisoner was following me. I just touched him with my foot, and the prisoner turned round and kicked me between my legs. I went into the place where we stay over night, and then I began to bleed rather badly. I did not think it was so serious then; but in the night I found I was bleeding badly. I don't think it was malice, but rather a frolic, for there was nothing wrong between us before.'*[39]

John Davies

In June of 1812 a man named John Davies was descending a rope within one of the mine shafts when he fell fifty yards to his death. The inquest determined that the rope had not been properly secured before John began to climb down it. Grimly a newspaper reported how John was *'dashed to pieces'*[40] without any chance of surviving the fall. He was buried in Llandudno on 25th June 1812.

An article reporting the incident in *The North Wales Gazette* suggested that *'the care of those ropes were submitted to the management of one man'*[41] so perhaps, though we will never know, John's death may have prevented the death of other miners both in Llandudno and further afield with lessons having been learnt in the hindsight of his passing. It would be nice to think that his death encouraged other mines to change their practises for to ensure that all ropes were in a safe condition before use and that checks were made on whether they were fixed before descent.

---

36 *North Wales Weekly News* – Friday 11 December 1896
37 *North Wales Weekly News* – Friday 11 December 1896
38 *North Wales Times* – Saturday 23 January 1897
39 *North Wales Times* – Saturday 12 December 1896
40 *The Cambrian* – 4th July 1812
41 *North Wales Gazette* – 25th June 1812

John Davies

This may look like a typo, a mistake of repetition in my text, especially given the close proximity in years and identical name to the man listed previously, but sadly it is not. The only thing repeated here is history.

Born in 1778 John Davies lived at Bryn Glas in Llandudno and is the first death listed in the town's printed parish register. His name at the top of the page and death is cited as '*killed in the Mine Work*'. Christopher Draper in his book '*Llandudno Before The Hotels*' expands on this, stating his cause of death was in a roof collapse at the mine.

John was buried in Llandudno on February 3rd 1813, he was thirty-five years old.

John Griffiths, circa 1860.
Image with thanks to Conwy Archive.

John Griffiths

Described by chronicler Thomas Rowlands as an '*industrious and godly person... for whom everyone had a good word*', John Griffiths knew a great amount about misery and loss too.

Born in Anglesey in 1788, it was the call of the Llandudno copper mines that drew him to the other side of the Straits. Once in Llandudno he had a different sort of calling, that of the religious kind and was baptised becoming one of the Creuddyn Baptists in 1818. He had married a woman named Margaret Hughes and they had two children, John and Elizabeth. It seems for several short years the family enjoyed a certain amount of happiness and stability. John was employed at one of the mines and Margaret had a son and a daughter to dote on.

This period of bliss was not to last. In January of 1819 his two children John, aged four and Elizabeth, aged three, died in a house fire. That evening John and Margaret had left their home, locking the door behind them in order to attend a local religious meeting leaving John and Elizabeth at home at Pen y Buarth. In the interests of not viewing this through twenty-first century eyes and forming an opinion outside of its historical context, I wish to add that during these times this was an entirely commonplace practice for parents to do, and presumably they felt that their children would be safer should they be locked inside their home. Sadly though this could not have been further from the reality of how events unfolded that tragic January evening. During the absence of their parents, somehow the home caught fire and reportedly nothing was left of the house but ashes. The sheer terror that must have coursed through John as he and his wife headed for home that evening, seeing their house ablaze and knowing their two small children were inside. The parish record of John and Elizabeth's burials simply says '*burnt to death*'. John and Margaret's loss and level of grief is unimaginable and the whole community was shaken. It seems that John's faith helped him with this huge weight of sadness, in 1822 he began preaching and eventually became a minister. Alas, more heartbreak was on its way.

In 1825 his wife Margaret died leaving John a widower. Finding himself suffering yet another bereavement he must have resolved not to bear his grief alone as in 1826 he remarried, a woman named Catherine Ellis, and they went on to have several children, perhaps partially healing the wounds in his heart.

John was a very skilled preacher and to aid him in this the Church purchased for him a pony to more easily and quickly get to those that needed to hear him speak. It is said that John delighted in the telling of a story of one such occasion that he was due to preach, but had no idea of the directions of the place he was supposed to preach at, fortunately the animal in question had been there before, and so his trusty steed took him there herself![42] On his death in 1864 it was suggested that had he been able to devote more time to '*delve into the mines of the gospel instead of the copper mines of Llandudno*'[43] few would

42 *The History of the Llandudno Baptists – Trustees of the Tabernacl circa* 1969 - 1972
43 *Seren Cymru* – 1st January 1864

exceed him in his knowledge of the former. It is perhaps Thomas Rowlands though that best summarises the reverence that people in Llandudno had for this man when he said '*I feel that we walk on hallowed ground in mentioning his name. With his long white hair, a glorious crown on his head, his serious appearance, his slow steady gait and his faultless life*'. What a beautiful way to be remembered.

David Hughes

Like other miners in this book, David Hughes tragically lost his life in the course of duties beyond mining activities.

The railway's arrival in North Wales posed challenges, one of which was how to pass through the mountains of Penmaenmawr, and so the engineer company granted the contract to construct this tunnel found themselves without alternative than to blast through the hard

An image of the area adjacent to the railway line at Penmaenmawr before the construction of the A55, and in the distance just visible, the Penmaenbach Railway Tunnel, an engineering feat that cost David Hughes his life. Image with thanks to Conwy Archive, CCBC.

rock. Of around 200 men working on the project David Hughes was one. Like other ex-copper miners from Llandudno David worked early and late, blasting rock with gunpowder to create a tunnel of 718 yards (656 metres) in length.

However, one August night in 1846 David was killed in a blasting accident leaving behind a large family. Some of his co-workers who were caught up in the blast suffered injuries such as burns and broken bones, but they escaped the incident with their lives. David sadly was not as lucky. He is the only recorded fatality in the construction of the project which by all other regards was described as being '*remarkably fortunate*'[44].

David gave his life in the course of his labours improving the transport links along the North Wales coast, which, as the tourism industry grew, would become increasingly important. Mourned by his family, colleagues and community, newspapers of the time defined him as being '*a very industrious and well conducted man*'[45].

Hugh Hughes

Over the centuries Great Orme has tragically claimed many lives including that of Llandudno miner Hugh Hughes. As he walked to work one November morning in 1847 alongside his colleagues Hugh lost his footing on a cliff edge and fell, hitting rocks as he slipped, before landing in the sea and the waves swallowed him. Though other miners were walking with Hugh that day and had witnessed the tragic events unfold before them, it all happened so quickly that they could do nothing to intervene.[46] No doubt what they saw left them with lasting emotional effects.

His devastated friends searched for his body and it was retrieved from the sea later that day. An inquest was held into his death a couple of days later and he was buried in St George's Churchyard on November 27th.

Sadly little else exists in record of Hugh's life other than his untimely death on his short commute from his home at Brynhyfryd on Great Orme to where he worked, a journey he had probably made countless times before and should have continued to do so far beyond his thirty-seven years.

44 *North Wales Weekly News* – Thursday 26 February 1976
45 *Chester Chronicle* – Friday 21 August 1846
46 *North Wales Chronicle* – Tuesday 30 November 1847

Joseph Jones

It was not just to the betterment of Llandudno that the miners were able to turn the engineering skills that they had previously applied at the mines, but further afield too. In 1846 the erection of the Conwy Railway Bridge began and many workers with the appropriate skill set were required. One such Llandudno miner that came forward to apply his expertise to the construction of this new bridge was Joseph Jones, a married man supporting a very large family of eleven children. Given Joseph's experience as a boatman combined with his mining knowledge, he was an ideal candidate. The project would have been very exciting, a tubular railway bridge to span the River Conwy, which was being designed by civil engineer Robert Stevenson.

However, on the evening of Friday February 18th 1848 at 10pm, Joseph Jones lost his life in the bringing about of this construction. In preparation to float the first of the tubes, he and another three men were aboard a boat, including a man named David Simon, when their boat encountered a rope that was stretched across the water, the force of this collision knocked him and David overboard. David was saved, but Joseph, though a strong swimmer, was seen to be taken by the force of the river's current and he sank beneath the waters. A crew sailed off to where they had last seen Joseph in an attempt to save his life, but they never found him.

His wife Jane lived a difficult life thereafter, left with many children from the ages of two upwards. Fortunately, several of her children were already in employment at the mines, so were able to provide some household financial income. Jane had been married to Joseph since 1818 and now approaching fifty, had to support and raise her family alone. During the next few years she struggled, on the 1861 census she is listed as being a pauper, but as the years progressed her conditions improved and she found work as a Housekeeper. But perhaps her and Joseph's biggest legacy to Llandudno was their children, including their sons Hugh and Richard who would go onto work on the town's lifeboat, no doubt largely motivated by the loss of their own father from drowning, that they sought to prevent other families from

Conwy Tubular Bridge
(Image: Picken, Thomas, d. 1891, lithographer through Creative Commons)

suffering that same loss.

Completed in 1849 and described at the time as one of '*those stupendous triumphs of science*'[47] the Conwy Tubular Bridge still carries trains today and it stands as a monument not just to the work of Stevenson, but all that toiled in its construction, including Joseph Jones.

47 *Manchester Times* – Wednesday 18 July 1849

Thomas Jones

Thomas was born in Llandudno in 1814, the son of Owen and Jane Jones. In 1837 he married a woman named Elizabeth and the pair went onto have children together. Sadly Thomas and Elizabeth lost several of their children in childhood including Ellenor and William who died only a matter of weeks apart. In 1849 Ellenor died on the 30th April aged two and less than a month later their son William died on the 23rd May aged ten. Both children were buried in the same grave in St George's Churchyard.

On the 1841, 1851 and 1861 censuses Thomas is listed as being a miner in the town, however by 1871 this had changed. Thomas' occupation was then listed as a town porter. No doubt the better prospects of being a porter, ferrying luggage to and from the train station was much more lucrative now that Llandudno was established as a seaside resort, than the hard work and toil that the ever declining local copper mining opportunities afforded.

In 1886, at the age of seventy-two Thomas was one of the oldest porters working in the town and was becoming increasingly infirm. Heading off to the train station ready to load his handcart on one fateful day, early in the morning of Wednesday 18th August 1886, Thomas was to meet with his end.

Thomas Jones' headstone in St Tudno's Churchyard, the headstone he shares with John Jones who died in 1811.

Coming from the slaughterhouse was John Roberts, a boy of sixteen who had recently begun employment with a local butcher. John was driving a horse and shandry, and at the inquest that followed it was estimated that he had been travelling at approximately eight miles per hour, a slow trot, not deemed especially fast for a Llandudno trader. As Roberts turned into Augusta Street he struck Thomas Jones, knocking him down and running over him. Described at the inquest as having been '*stupefied*'[48] by the accident, Thomas was taken home to Bodafon Row by local man Robert Roberts. Robert stated that Thomas had declined the offer to be taken to the hospital, preferring to be nursed at home. At home he was attended by a doctor who reported that Thomas had suffered bruising and broken ribs. Thomas' neighbour Ellen Williams looked after him as he died, and she was also present at the inquest, stating that during his decline Thomas had no recollection of the collision.

The evening that followed the accident Thomas died as a result of his injuries. Roberts was charged with manslaughter, with no witnesses having heard him shout to Thomas to ask him to move out of the way and given that the road was wide enough to pass, it was determined that Roberts must have been distracted at the time of the crash. Immediately after the incident John Roberts said that he had been unable to control the horse he was driving and ask it to stop in time, however a witness present at the inquest who knew the horse cast doubt on that and said the horse in question was old and quiet tempered. Ultimately when the case came to trial in the October, Roberts was acquitted, owing to '*considerable discrepancy as to the rate in which the prisoner was driving and the position of the deceased handcart on the street*'[49].

Thomas was buried in St Tudno's churchyard and his funeral was well attended. His headstone reads:

In health and strength he left his home
Not thinking that death was near;
It pleased the lord to bid him come,
And in his presence to appear.

A few lines that gain extra poignancy when one knows of the cause of Thomas' death. Thomas lies in the same grave as a man named John Jones, the headstone inscription stating he was a former agent

48 *The North Wales Chronicle and Advertiser for the Principality* – 28th August 1886
49 *North Wales Chronicle* – Saturday 30 October 1886

The metal grill covering Copper Ddu Shaft (Vivian's Shaft) as it appears today. Likely to have been the shaft of Old Mine that William Foulkes fell fifty yards down – and survived to tell the tale!

of the copper mines at Conistone [sic]. John predeceased Thomas by more than seventy years but given that they share a surname and a grave it is possible they are related, but how I have been unable to determine as of yet.

William Foulkes

Some miners were lucky and survived extremely close calls during their daily toils underground, and William Foulkes is one such fortunate man. As a miner at Old Mine on the morning of Saturday the 11th January 1845 he had an accident that he was extremely lucky to survive. Descending the ladder in one of Old Mine's shafts, as he would have routinely done many times before, he missed his footing and fell a reported fifty yards (almost forty-six metres). Given that it was January it is likely that the accident was caused by a ladder that was wet or icy.

His fellow miners must have thought that he was to be another sad statistic in Victorian mining deaths, however William was certainly a survivor. Described in *The North Wales Chronicle* as having been knocked unconscious, he was '*picked up*'[50] and treated for bleeding from several

50 *North Wales Chronicle* – Tuesday 14 January 1845

places on his head as well as an '*indentation*' of the skull. The newspaper holds a frivolous tone, calling this indentation '*a lasting memento of his morning's adventure*'[51]. I'm not sure that William would have called it that! Less sensationally this incident was also reported in *The Mining Journal* a few days later as a story with a positive outcome, William having survived without '*serious injury*'[52].

Sixty-six years later former miner John Williams reflected on how treacherous the ladders were at Old Mine; '*I know of two men who fell down the ladders of No. 2 Shaft* [Copper Ddu Shaft, known as Vivian's Shaft today] *and were badly hurt. They got well and worked again*'. It seems likely that William Foulkes is one of the men that John was referring to.

John Roberts

(Due to several John Roberts matching the description in age, birthplace and occupation living in Llandudno at that time I have been unable to ascertain the particulars of his life, but wanted to include the following account in this book).

Born in Amlwch like so many others in this book, in 1844 during his daily work at Old Mine John had a terrible accident.

Working at the capstan with a few other miners John got his head caught between one of its arms and a fixed post. *The North Wales Chronicle* said '*his skull was dreadfully and extensively fractured, a portion the size of a crown piece completely beaten in: and pressing on the brain*'[53]. Absolutely horrifying injuries for him to have suffered and his fellow miners to have witnessed. Help was promptly obtained for him in the form of Conwy surgeon Mr. Hope Jones and he swiftly operated, removing part of John's skull.

Despite his horrific ordeal the prognosis seemed very positive as it was reported that he was '*getting on exceedingly well*'[54]. A few days later *The Mining Journal* wrongly reported of his death, with a

51 *North Wales Chronicle* – Tuesday 14 January 1845
52 *The Mining Journal* – 18th January 1845
53 *North Wales Chronicle* – Tuesday 14 January 1845
54 *North Wales Chronicle* – Tuesday 14 January 1845

retraction being published in the following issue '*we are glad to find that our information was incorrect, and that Roberts is fast recovering from the effects of his dreadful injuries*'[55]. A happy ending after all!

John Williams

There have been many shipwrecks off the cliffs of Great Orme over the years. One of the more famous ones is that of the Hornby on New Year's Day in 1824.

The Hornby left Liverpool bound for Rio de Janeiro, carrying £60,000 worth of cargo, but as it approached the coast of Anglesey was caught in strong gales and for two days the crew struggled in the storm. It was suggested to Wade, the brig's captain, that they make for Beaumaris for safety, dock and set sail once the storm subsided, but it is said that he responded with the remark that he would rather be at sea forever than go there. Unfortunately, that decision was to prove fatal to all but one of those aboard.

Prior to only ten minutes before the Hornby's collision with the Orme the crew apparently had no awareness that they were sailing so close to land until it was

The cliffs of Great Orme, with the lighthouse in the far distance that was erected to prevent such tragedies as The Hornby, photographed June 2018.

55 *The Mining Journal* – 25th January 1845

too late. The only survivor out of the crew of fourteen and two passengers was lookout John Williams. During the vessel's final moments Captain Wade had asked John to loosen the jib, but as he went to do so Williams looked down and saw that they were above rocks and found himself thrown upon them. The *Liverpool Advertiser* published Williams' account of his ordeal, in which he described how from The Hornby he had dropped onto some rocks, but upon landing lost sight of the brig. As soon as he was able he climbed the cliffs and went running across the Orme desperate to find someone who might be able to assist. At approximately 5am he found the copper miners assembling for the working day. By the miners Williams was initially disbelieved, as they thought that the likelihood of him being able to climb the section of the cliff face he had described impossible and his story too outlandish, but a group of them made for the site of the wreck, and although they found some of the remains of the vessel, of the Hornby's crew or passengers there was no trace.

The gap in the rocks where part of the vessel was forced into by the strength of the storm was named Hornby Cave, and that name still is connected to this site today.

John Williams remained in Llandudno for the rest of his life and worked as a copper miner, finding employment where he had once found refuge and sought rescue for his doomed shipmates. It is said that in his later years John would regale tourists with his '*miraculously*'[56] fortunate story of survival.

Owen Williams

During the peak years of the Llandudno copper mining industry the mines offered financial safety for the population of the town, ensuring that they could continue to put food on the table. During the Napoleonic Wars for Owen Williams the mines also offered safety in a very physical sense.

Owen was born in 1789 and during his youth the Napoleonic Wars were taking place. There was a general concern abroad in the town that the French may invade via Llandudno, with some locals taking measures to defend themselves, Owen's

56 *London Courier and Evening Gazette* – Monday 12 January 1824

own father is recorded as having been seen sharpening a pitchfork to fashion into a weapon. This is likely to be what prompted Owen to leave Llandudno and enlist with the army, and so as a soldier he was bound for the continent. However by the time he had arrived at Dover ready to set sail, he had become weak and frail. Evidently feeling in his weakened state unable to fight, he decided to desert the army, returning the over three hundred miles home. Along the way back to North Wales he begged for food and lived on his wits, and by the time he arrived in his hometown of Llandudno he was reportedly in a very sorry state of health and wellbeing. His original infirmities made worse by the long journey and little food. His family's heart must have gone out to him, as whether they knew it or not, if discovered Owen was likely to be shot as his penalty for desertion.

Time passed and Owen returned to work at the mines, falling into a steady routine of daily life. However, soon after there became talk in the village that soldiers were staying locally, and Owen guessed correctly that they had finally caught up with him and were going to see that he was punished accordingly. Being a miner, and knowing that those underground passages could hide him when the soldiers came looking, he spent the daylight hours underground, hiding away, and must have been terrified. Robert Williams, his protective father, decided to take the bull by the horns and see if the soldiers were indeed looking for his son and slipped into the Kings Head where he knew they would be. However, it seems that there was a strong familial resemblance between father and son as the soldiers immediately recognised Robert as the father of Owen. When questioned about his son initially Robert denied having any relationship to Owen, but eventually he admitted to being his father. Seemingly Owen's fate was sealed and he was to be shot for desertion. What happened instead was the soldiers declared that they had become fond of Owen and had no intention of removing him from his home, vowing that they would not give him away to their superiors. Owen was sent for and after arriving at the Kings Head, at which point he must have been fearful that he was soon to meet his end, a '*jollification*'[57] took place at the pub,

57 *Llandudno Advertiser and List of Visitors* – 27th March 1909

and the soldiers, true to their word, did not arrest Owen. Instead, Owen continued working as a copper miner, married in 1813 and had a family, on the 1841 census he is listed as living at Min Don with his wife Jane and their six children. Owen's amiability saved his life, and this admiration for Owen was not limited to those he had met in the army, he and his family were described by Thomas Rowlands as being '*eminently respectable*'.

The Innovators and The Esteemed

Joseph Hobson

In January of 1869 it was reported in local press that miner Joseph Hobson, having dedicated his spare time to exploring the Orme for decades in the hope of finding a new vein of copper, had finally done just that. This vein that he had discovered was reputed to contain the '*richest of copper in quality that has ever been discovered on the mountain*'[58] (*Caernarvon & Denbigh Herald - Saturday 23 January 1869*). It was anticipated that the find would go on to procure him a great amount of wealth, along with David Lloyd, the leaseholder of Old Mine at that time. For both men this must have seemed like the answer to many prayers. Old Mine had become increasingly unprofitable and at this time Joseph, still working as a miner in his seventies, might have been able to look forward to a more relaxed old age and with this promise of wealth, a comfortable retirement.

This vein went on to be named '*Hobson's Vein*' and was apparently four and a half feet thick, with other intersecting veins beneath it. The entrance was at a place called Hugh Hughes' Pit Cae Gron and it was located eighty yards from Copper Ddu (Vivian's) Shaft, 150 yards from Owens' Shaft and 150 yards from Treweek's Shaft.

The fate of the vein remains unclear, but it seems unlikely that it reaped Hobson any of the rewards he had hoped for. Old Mine continued in unprofitability and Hobson's Vein, like a lot of Great Orme's history, today remains buried beneath the landscape.

Whatever happened to the vein, Joseph sadly did not live long enough to find out. After spending years of his life looking for the vein he was convinced he would one day find, he died in the June following its discovery. From the words etched on his headstone it is evident that Joseph was an educated man, for it says that he had '*served in the educational profession in Wales for many years*' and he was described in local press as having been '*industrious*' and that he had possessed a '*practical knowledge*'[59] of Great Orme.

---

58 *Caernarvon & Denbigh Herald* – Saturday 23 January 1869

59 *Caernarvon & Denbigh Herald* – Saturday 23 January 1869

The estimated location of Hobson's Vein, photographed prior to the construction of the upper track of the Great Orme Tramway, which opened in 1903.
Image obtained with thanks to Tom Parry.

Hugh Hughes

Born to William and Margaret Hughes in Llaneilian on Anglesey, Hugh married a woman called Catherine (known locally in Llandudno as 'Kitty'). By the time of the birth of the couple's child Edward in 1817 they had moved to Llandudno and were living at Llwyn Helig and Hugh was supporting his family working as a miner. When their son Robert was baptised in 1822 they had moved to one of the houses at Tai Newyddion. On the 1841 census Hugh is the head of a household where all the male occupants are miners; his four sons, Edward, Owen, Robert and William, all having followed their father into pursuing a career in copper mining. This was a career that was obviously paying well for the Hughes family, as on the 1851 census they were able to afford to have a servant, Jane Williams, in their employment, who lives with the family, along with Hugh's granddaughter, Catherine Lewis. By 1851 though, Hugh

Catherine "Kitty" Hughes' headstone in St George's Churchyard.

The pockmarks of Bryniau Poethion, 1849's 'Welsh California'. Was one of these shown Hugh Hughes' Pit?
Image with thanks to Great Orme Mines.

Bryniau Poethion 'Welsh California' seen from a distance.
Image with thanks to Great Orme Mines.

had lost his wife, Kitty having died a year earlier. Her headstone, now lying flat in St George's Churchyard shows of the affection between the pair, describing her as having been Hugh's '*beloved*' wife.

Thomas Rowlands shared his recollections of Hugh as '*an old straightbacked manly figure who prided himself on his great strength. He was seen in Penmorfa to grip the two handles of a wheelbarrow and to lift and turn it over his head, an achievement beyond the capabilities of any other Llandudno resident*'. It sounds as though Hugh was Llandudno's strongest man!

Another curious mention of Hugh Hughes comes from an article in the *Caernarvon and Denbigh Herald* relating to the copper vein that Joseph Hobson discovered in 1868, that said the entrance to said vein was at '*Hugh Hughes's Pit Cae Gron*'[60]. The pit mentioned in the article may be referring to one of the pock marks on Bryniau Poethion on Great Orme, that were dug during 1849 in a time of Llandudno's history that came to be known as 'Welsh California'. This was a time when people flocked to the town to prospect to find their own vein of copper ore, in the hope of being financially set for life. This prospecting was concentrated in a relatively small area of Great Orme, just adjacent to where the upper section of the Great Orme Tramway is today, and the hillside in that area still bears the scars from this intensive period of prospecting. It sounds like Hugh Hughes was one of the many that dug one of these holes in a desperate and frenzied search for his fortune. Unfortunately none of the pits came to much, but left a permanent mark across the face of the Orme, evidence of just how frenzied that pursuit of copper ore was. Though given that Hobson's Vein was very close to Hugh Hughes' Pit, perhaps Hugh was only feet away from making his fortune, for which the old proverb about '*a miss being as good as a mile*' comes to mind!

Richard Hughes

Described as having been a man with a '*natural ability for surveying and engineering*'[61] Richard was born in Anglesey and moved to Llandudno in the 1830s to work in the town's copper mines. Soon

60 *Caernarvon & Denbigh Herald* – Saturday 23 January 1869
61 *Llandudno Advertiser and List of Visitors* – 24th June 1897

Richard Hughes posing in his mining attire at LaRoche (The Rock) Studios.
Image courtesy of Conwy Archive Service, Conwy County Borough Council.

after he met and married Elizabeth Jones of Pwllygwichiad Farm and by 1841 the pair resided at The Miners Arms, a prominent gathering place for locals who were employed in the town's copper mining industry. As the family grew they moved to the Morfa before finally they settled at Madoc Street.

Like many other of his copper mining contemporaries in the town, Richard was a man of religion and in 1840 was baptised in the sea of Llandudno before eventually going on to become a Welsh Baptist Deacon and a treasurer of the Tabernacl Chapel.

Appearing on the 1841, 1851, 1861, and 1871 censuses as a copper miner, like many other miners he was ultimately drawn to the town's newer and increasingly more lucrative economy, the tourism industry. Turning his engineering talents and skills to tourism he became a pioneer in the introduction and development of the bathing machine in the resort, a feature that would become iconic of Victorian Llandudno and one that lasted into the twentieth century. One of Richard's engineering efforts that most definitely stood the test of time is Marine Drive. In 1878 the road that he had been one of the three contractors hired to build opened. Now, almost a hundred and fifty years later this road remains a huge Llandudno attraction, with thousands of visitors per year visiting the town to drive, cycle and walk the three and a half miles of unparalleled views. What Richard helped to create is now also the setting for several sports race events, including rallying, cycling and running.

As he aged though he suffered from illness and withdrew from some of his bigger commitments in the town and died in June 1897. He was buried in St Tudno's Churchyard on Great Orme on Saturday 19th June where a large number of mourners turned out to bid farewell to a man that was very widely respected and would be sorely missed.

As pictured in the 1980s, Shafft yr Odyn, an old well that Thomas Rowlands recalled as being adjacent to the end of Reuben Jones' garden, close to Ysgol San Siôr.
Photo with thanks to the Great Orme Exploration Society.

Reuben Jones

Reuben Jones was born in December of 1805 in Llanasa and married Mary Jones of Cwm in 1836. By 1839 they had moved to Llandudno, and as a married couple before long they started a family, Joseph had been the first to be born in 1838, followed by Sarah and Mary Anne in 1840 and 1850 respectively.

The family lived in a cottage on Cwlach Street and for many years he worked as a copper miner. By 1861 though, Reuben had embarked on a new career, and was listed as a House Carpenter on that year's census. In 1871 he was earning a living as a Lodging Housekeeper at Bedford House, his changing careers reflecting the growth and development of the town and Reuben had adapted to the new Llandudno, recognising its modern direction as a seaside resort.

Away from the mines Reuben held several positions within Llandudno, one of which was as a founder member of the town's English Congregational Chapel, where for many years he served in the position of Deacon.

In early 1877 he suffered a personal loss, Mary, his wife of forty years, died and in the summer of 1886 a further sadness when his daughter Sarah also passed away. He carried on running Bedford House, and on the 1891 census is joined by the company of his daughter Mary Anne and is the employer of one domestic servant.

Reuben lived a long life and, at the time of his death on 6th May 1897, it was stated that he had been the oldest inhabitant in the town, reported as taking regular exercise until only a short time before his passing. His obituary describes him as being a prominent figure and highly respected amongst a wide circle. He was laid to rest in a private funeral at St Tudno's Churchyard in an oak coffin with brass mountings.

His legacy of service to Llandudno and its people would continue in his descendants and wider family. In January of 1887 Reuben's grandson had been born and Joseph and his wife Mary gave him the same name as his paternal grandfather. Growing up seeing the eminent example of his grandfather before him, no doubt Reuben Dexter Jones took inspiration from his ancestor and in 1957 went onto receive an OBE from the Queen at Buckingham Palace in recognition of fifty-six years of faithful service in local government. Reuben Dexter had successfully taken over the mantle from his copper mining ancestor, who had sowed the seeds of modern Llandudno over a century before.

Richard Jones

In 1824 at the age of twenty, Richard Jones was drawn to Llandudno, like others, from his place of birth which for him was in Brynsiencyn on Anglesey, for employment at one of the then booming copper mines. In 1851 he was still working as a copper miner, to support the growing family he was raising with his wife Grace. The census of that year also shows that he was accompanied by his two sons, Hugh and Robert, in the same line of employment, who had chosen to join their father as Llandudno copper miners.

With the gradual decline in profitability and output of the Llandudno mines Richard channelled his other talents. Sometime between 1851 and 1861 his time at the mines came to an end as he is listed on the 1861 census as being a shoemaker, which was his occupation for the next twenty years, during which time he lived on Madoc Street and Back Madoc Street.

Richard was a well-read man, said to be extremely knowledgeable about the bible, and was a Calvinistic deacon for over fifty years until his death, by which time he was the district's oldest deacon at the advanced age of eighty-three. His knowledge was not restricted to theology, he is described as having had a keen interest in current affairs, as a Liberal man who advocated reform and the making of a better world. Very appropriate then that he lived in nineteenth century Llandudno, where all around him he would have seen change, as the town moved from being one of industrial toil to a place built for the purposes of relaxation and leisure.

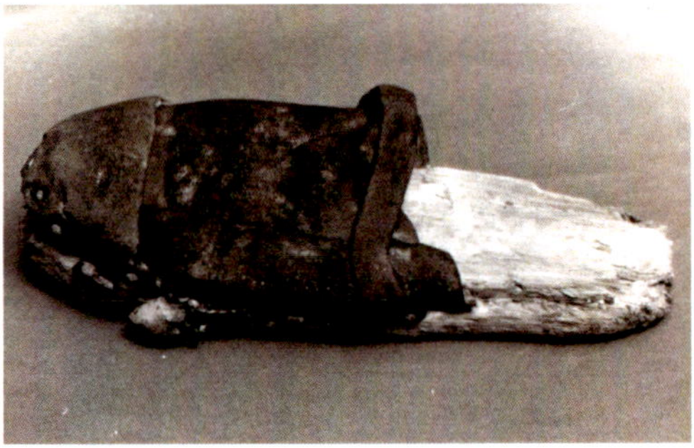

A miner's clog found in the Great Orme workings, possibly crafted by Richard Jones or one such shoemaker like him.

He died at home in October of 1887 following a short illness and was buried in St Tudno's Churchyard, where the ceremony was attended by a large group of mourners. Richard played an important part in Llandudno, advocating liberalism in a quiet '*unobtrusive*'[62] way, and keeping the members of the community shod. In a town undergoing a large amount of structural building and economic change, the importance of having the basics – such as reliable footwear, cannot be underestimated!

Edward Owen

Edward was born in Llandudno to Lewis and Elinor Owen and was baptised in April 1816. As a lifelong resident of Llandudno's Great Orme it is no surprise that Edward found work in the copper mines, and like other miners in Llandudno at that time he was also a farmer.

In 1839 he had married Margaret Ellis and later moved to Pen y Ogof with his wife and they would go onto have eight children together in eighteen years. By 1851 the family had settled at Pyllau where Edward and Margaret remained for the rest of their lives.

Apparently a man of cheer and warmth, Thomas Rowlands documented that when he passed Pyllau Farm he would frequently see '*smiles on the faces of Edward and Margaret Owen*' and that they had '*many interesting old stories*' of the town to tell. How wonderful it would have been to

Edward Owen, image used with kind permission of his direct descendant, Norman Rogers-Jones.

62 *Caernarvon & Denbigh Herald* – Friday 14 October 18878

sit and listen to those stories!

In 1853 there was a strike at Old Mine following a disagreement between the miners and the mine's new owners. The new owners of the mine, John Taylor and Sons, demanded of the men an eight hour working day, but much of the workforce, like Edward, had farming commitments to attend to, which they had previously fitted around a six hour working day. The strike lasted most of that year. One wonders how Edward felt during this time, struggling with the fear of how he would feed his family during the period of industrial action, and how difficult it must have been to return to work and maintain his farm with the miners having lost their case and left with little choice but to agree to the eight hour working day.

Edward died in February 1863 at the age of forty-six, and was buried in St Tudno's Churchyard. Margaret outlived him by forty years and continued to raise their large family. She would come to be known locally as '*Mrs Owen Pyllau*'[63]. Upon her death her and Edward's children were described as being '*among the most successful business men in Llandudno*'[64] (*Carnarvon and Denbigh Herald and North and South Wales Independent.*) She was buried alongside her husband. Their headstone spells Edward's name as 'Edwart Owen Pyllau'.

Michael Powell

Michael Powell and his twin brother, Harry, were born in Amlwch in 1807, the sons of Hugh and Anne Powell. Sorrowfully like many children of that time, Harry sadly did not survive infancy. Michael married Elizabeth Williams and the pair went onto have several children. By 1841 Michael was a Llandudno copper miner, and he and his family lived at Pen y Gwaith, Llandudno. Pen y Gwaith (sometimes referred to as Llwyn Helyg) was located where now is Maes y Facrell Nature Reserve (adjacent to the Bronze Age mining heritage attraction complex).

Michael's role in the town was not limited to his industrial labours either, he was also known as '*the old respected deacon*' (T. Rowlands *Adgofion am Landudno*) of the Wesleyan Church. He died in May of

63 *Carnarvon and Denbigh Herald and North and South Wales Independent* – 13th February 1903
64 *Carnarvon and Denbigh Herald and North and South Wales Independent* – 3th February 1903

The ruins of Pen y Gwaith, Great Orme

1854 at the age of forty-seven. The ruins of where Michael once lived now stand as an echo of Llandudno's mining past. Llwyn Helyg at Pen y Gwaith is gradually being reclaimed by nature, but by standing and viewing the remains of this ghost street one can almost imagine to hear the chatter and laughter of Michael and his family.

Robert Roberts

Born in 1825, Robert Roberts who was apparently a strong and agile sort of man, began his working life as a copper miner, but before old age he would turn his hand to a great many different careers, challenges and tasks. A man of many skills, after mining Robert worked in various professions, and was a very talented businessman. He became a butcher, and keeper of horses for leasing to wealthy visitors to the town. In a time long before motorised vehicles, the tourists of Llandudno would have relied heavily on renting equines in order to do their sightseeing. Robert kept extremely good quality horses and ponies, and as such he attracted business from the nobility, who would seek him out for his trusty steeds. Robert established a great relationship the visitors to the town, with whom he is described as having been a '*favourite*'[65]. Tourists were likely encouraged to make return visits because of the reliability of Robert Roberts, in the knowledge that he

65 *The Weekly News and Visitors' Chronicle for Colwyn Bay Colwyn Llandrillo Conway Deganwy and Neighbourhood* – 5th July 1907 (North Wales Edition)

would source for them the best horses that they required.

Equally as popular amongst his fellow residents, in 1889 he was elected a member of the Board of Commissioners and for the last twenty-five years of his life was a member of the Tabernacl Welsh Baptist Chapel, where he was a deacon.

When he died in 1907 at the grand age of eighty-two and was buried in St Tudno's Churchyard, Llandudno felt the loss not just of one of their loyal characters and constant community members, but grieved for one of the last connections to a bygone time, before the town rebranded as a holiday destination. For many of the town's residents Robert Roberts was a reminder of a simpler time in Llandudno's past, when the village was held together through mining, farming, fishing and worship. Now that '*another of the lines of the days when Llandudno was a fishing hamlet*'[66] had been severed, the memory of those days was left in the charge of the increasingly few that remained alive to tell it.

Archibald and William Worthington

Centric to communities in Wales in the nineteenth century was the Church, and after a terrible storm in January of 1839 the roof of St Tudno's Church on Great Orme was left badly damaged, leaving it exposed to the elements, and with the decision having been made not to make the necessary repairs, the parishioners found themselves in need of a new Anglican church in which to worship.

Archibald and William were brothers and at that time joint leasees of Old Mine, (their father Samuel Worthington had taken out a lease in 1837 for the entire length of the natural lives of his sons). With the town in need of an Anglican place of worship, the English brothers financed the building of St George's Church on Church Walks.

In 1840 the building of the church was completed and services could commence following its consecration in August of that year, which was, according to *The North Wales Chronicle and Advertiser for the Principality*, attended by at least 700 people. On the day of the consecration,

66 *The Weekly News and Visitors' Chronicle for Colwyn Bay Colwyn Llandrillo Conway Deganwy and Neighbourhood* – 5th July 1907 (North Wales Edition)

the Bishop's arrival was announced, having robed at the residence of Archibald and William, and following the event he, the Dean of Bangor and Deputy Registrar, returned with the Worthingtons to their home for a light meal.

The newspaper describes a certain amount of reverent anticipation of this event by the people of Llandudno '*the different works were deserted by the miners, who appeared in their best apparel, and observed throughout the day the greatest propriety of conduct*'[67]. In a rather judging manner, the report on this event even goes as far as to say that amongst the miners no signs of alcohol intoxication were evident and sounds a little surprised at such! Clearly the reporter did not appreciate how God fearing the greater portion of the Llandudno miners were!

This new church had been built in an accessible part of town, as the mines had grown, Llandudno also had begun to expand in populous beyond the Great Orme itself, and now those that lived on the lower slopes could more easily attend a place of Anglican worship and pay their respects to their dead in the church's surrounding burial ground.

Following its construction, it took until 1862 for the church to be designated the Llandudno parish Church, and it continued to function as a place of worship until 2002. Since then, it has been privately owned and latterly the building functioned as a business centre. Perhaps not what the Worthington brothers had in mind when they financed the build, however their gift continues to play a part in modern Llandudno life.

The pair were also large financial contributors to a new line of road from Llanrhos to Llandudno, which opened on 30th July 1844, and it was remarked at the time that all those that witnessed its opening would remember the day forever. This road is another gift from the Worthingtons that Llandudno continues to enjoy!

Although the lease for Old Mine had been taken out by their father for their entire natural lives, in 1846 it was reassigned to the name of another, and the brothers disappeared from Llandudno's history. Perhaps this was for the reason that Don Smith in *The Great Orme Copper*

67 *North Wales Chronicle* – Tuesday 18 August 1840

St George's Church and Churchyard, 2021.

Mines speculates; '*Archibald and William may have sensed that the boom days had gone, never to return*'. Or perhaps it was simply for the most human of all reasons - pressing family issues potentially their father's declining health, that prompted the pair to leave Llandudno, especially given that their father died the following year. Whatever the reason for their departure, for the people of Llandudno for the duration that the pair were part of the town's copper mining story, Archibald and William had brought about changes and '*public improvements...in the most handsome manner*'[68].

68 *North Wales Chronicle* – Tuesday 06 August 1844

The Almost, But Should Never Be, Forgotten

As I have already mentioned, it is my intention to record the lives of all miners and their families, before too much time has lapsed, and the years have eroded all trace of them. In this chapter you will find the individuals on whom there is little documentary evidence of, beyond that they lived and died, and their remembrance in family trees around the world. Although their lives do not make for particularly sensational reading, the fact that they lived in the town, contributed to its economy and would have, though it is easy to forget from a twenty-first century standpoint, lived lives every bit as full, meaningful and worthy of being remembered as our own.

Thomas Lloyd's headstone at his final resting place in St George's Churchyard, Church Walks.

Thomas Lloyd

Thomas was born in the Welsh market town of Llanrwst in 1780 and later married a woman named Elinor. In time the pair moved to Llandudno and Thomas found work at one of the copper mines. At the time of the 1851 census, in his seventy-first year, he is listed as still working as a miner and living in the area Llwyn Helyg, Pen y Gwaith, in a property that once stood very close to where the Visitor Centre for the Great Orme Mines tour is today. Eventually this house would become engulfed in waste from the local mining activity.

Thomas Rowlands in '*Adgofion am*

Felicia Simpson's 1853 watercolour of the site of Old Mine. In the foreground is the engine house, with the brammock rods seen heading over the hillside in the distance. On the left of Pyllau Road (where the figures are pictured) is Llwyn Helyg, the area home to a number of miners, including Thomas Lloyd.

Landudno' mentions Thomas Lloyd and Elinor (also known as 'Ellen') but only in passing. Now little else remains of Thomas Lloyd but mere tiny echoes of his entire life. He was buried in St George's Churchyard on August 14th 1851.

Morgan Hughes

Earning a living in the nineteenth century was difficult and the toil that mining took on the physical self, particularly as a person aged, could make that even more challenging, and Morgan Hughes is an example of how this could place one in poverty.

Morgan was born in 1775 in Abertefi, Merionethshire but by 1841 he was living at an address listed as '*Mountain*' in Llandudno. It is unclear what brought him north to the town, but like others its likely it was employment opportunities at the copper mines. However in 1841 he was not working as a miner, but an agricultural labourer. Already approaching seventy years of age it seems likely that he had gone into farming following perhaps age and infirmity preventing him from continuing in the career he had come to the town for, as the 1851 census has him listed as being a '*pauper formerly miner*'. So it seems he had had to resort to agriculture when the toilsome nature of working in the bowels of the earth extracting copper ore was an occupation that had become too arduous to continue with as he aged. Given that he was categorised as a pauper on the 1851 census seems to suggest that the agricultural work had subsequently got too strenuous for him too, or perhaps the work became harder to come by, and so Morgan was dependant on charity and what little could be offered him. Nevertheless, he lived to the advanced age of eighty-three years old and died at his home at Pen y Buarth on 2nd December 1858 and was buried in St Tudno's churchyard. His headstone inscription reads; '*Morgan Hughes miner Llandudno Bu farw Rhag 2 1858 yn 83 oed*'.

Hugh Powell

The son of Michael (see chapter *The Innovators and The Esteemed*) and Elizabeth Powell, Hugh was born in Amlwch in 1828. His parents relocated the family to Llandudno where his father found work as a miner so it is not surprising that by the time the 1851 census was taken Hugh was employed as a miner also. At the age of twenty-four he married Barbara Burchell and they went onto have several children. However, during this period very few families were strangers to losing their children at a young age and in 1856 Hugh and Barbara lost their daughter Ellen when she was just three years old. With great sadness this was not to be the only loss of a child they would suffer, in 1876 they lost their son William, in 1890 daughter Louisa and 1892 another daughter, Catherine.

Only listed as a miner on the 1851 census, by the time the 1861 census was taken Hugh had changed occupations and

Hugh's wife Barbara standing outside their home. Picture used with kind permission of David Collins, direct descendant of Hugh and Barbara.

was working as a salesman and in 1871 a labourer. Hugh was continually adapting to the changing economy in Llandudno and learning new skills.

In 1900 Hugh lost his wife Barbara, and he went on to outlive her by three years. He died in 1903 having spent the last years of his life working as a casual labourer and living at the home he had lived in for many years during his married life, at The

Mount, Tan y Rogo Terrace (pictured). He is buried in St Tudno's churchyard.

Owen Thomas

In the nineteenth century Llandudno was to undergo a change, and those that were miners would learn to apply their skills to the development of the growing tourism industry to secure employment. Owen Thomas is unique in that he did not begin as a miner and then seek employment in another trade, but instead his career was to progress in the reverse. Born in 1809, on the 1851 census he is listed as a schoolmaster, later becoming a miner. It is unclear why he changed professions, particularly since the mining industry in Llandudno was at that time rapidly heading towards its twilight. Between those years he also had a change of residence from living on the Morfa to relocating to Madoc Street during the development of the town as a seaside resort. He died in February 1872, his wife Mary had predeceased him and he was survived by his daughter Margaret, the second daughter he had of that name, after losing their first child before her fifth birthday back in 1846.

The headstone of Owen Thomas' first daughter to bear the name of Marg in St George's Churchyard.

Richard Lester

Originally from Amlwch, Richard stands out on the census records for his listed occupation in 1851 which is '*copper ore dresser*'.

In 1841 Richard was working as a miner and living at Fferm Bach with his family, consisting of his wife Margaret and their children, sons William and Richard who were also miners, and daughter Margaret.

West Shore Boating Pond, where once was a Copper Pen, one of the sites where copper ore dressing took place.

The next ten years saw a change though, perhaps necessitated by his advancing years, by 1851 he is the only copper ore dresser listed on the census and has moved, now living at Capel Bach. Copper Ore Dressing was often done by women and children and involved separating the ore from the rock, washing it and preparing it for shipping and smelting. This would have been much less physically demanding than mining underground, and better suited to someone that may have had an infirmity or disability. This task was carried out on the Dressing Floors. One of which was located where the West Shore Boating Pond is now, then known as a 'Copper Pen' and one near Tŷ Gwyn Mine, close to where the pier is located today.

Richard is rare in that he had found himself working in an occupation of a predominantly female environment. He died in January of 1855 and was buried in Eglwys yn Rhos on the 27th of that month, at the age of seventy-three.

Griffith Owens

Described by Thomas Rowlands as a '*quiet Christian*' Griffith Owens was born in 1813. He was the elder brother of miner Edward Owen (see chapter *The Innovators and The Esteemed*), who were both the sons of Lewis and Elinor Owen. The Owen surname is sometimes recorded as either 'Owen' or 'Owens'. During his childhood he grew up on the Orme, but by the time of the 1841 census he was living with his brother and his sister-in-law at Pen-y-Ogof and was working as a copper miner. Shortly after this he met and married local woman and servant-maid Ann of Bodhyfryd, the daughter of Owen Williams, a labourer. In the years that followed the pair had several children, first a daughter, Elinor, and then Margaret, Owen, Ann and Jane. By the mid-1850s they were a happy family unit, living in their Tŷ Unno on the Morfa. However tragedy was to strike.

Four of the couple's children are listed in the parish's burial records in 1856. Margaret, Owen, Ann and Jane. All buried on the same day, March 9th 1856. It's unclear what devastating and terrible event occurred. Could they have drowned in a storm, having lived so close to the sea? Was it a house fire caused by a stray spark from the hearth or a fallen candle? A housefire had claimed the lives of fellow miner John Griffith's children, so did Llandudno see history repeat itself? Maybe it was disease that caused their deaths to occur in such a short space of time, the children all having contracted the same illness. This seems quite likely as all the deaths recorded on that page of the parish register are of children. Did some destructive and virulent childhood disease sweep through the village? Whatever the cause Griffith and Ann must have been devastated. Their hearts ripped out, their family destroyed in such a short space of time. Did Griffith and Ann find solace in their Christian faith? I hope so, as even for the nineteenth century when the threat of danger and disease was never too far away, losing so many children in such a short space of time was rare.

By the time the 1861 census was taken the family were healing to some extent,

Madoc Street in the early 1920s, perhaps not so different from the Madoc Street Griffith knew in the 1880s. Image used with thanks to the Conwy County Archive, CCBC.

they had relocated to 17 Madoc Street. Their eldest child Elinor, by then aged seventeen, was living with her parents at home, and had been joined by younger siblings Owen, Edward and Margaret. It is poignant to note that two of these children bear the same names of those children lost, named after their much loved and lost brother and sister. Griffith was still supporting his family by working as a copper miner, and Ann was substituting that income with work as a laundress. However, a change of career was on the horizon for Griffith.

When the 1871 census was taken Griffith was listed as a Grocer, and he, Ann and three of their children Owen, Edward and Margaret, were living at 24 Madoc Street and they also had a servant living with them named Ellen Goosey. It is evident that this line of work suited Griffith and that in it he became successful, as on the 1881 census he is listed as a Grocer and Baker and Owen had joined his father in the same occupation. At their premises of 'Gronant House' they also employed a waitress, Elizabeth Williams. The need for a waitress suggests that the business was busy, and as by 1881 Llandudno was firmly established as a holiday resort, the need for bakers and grocers was an essential part of that. Hotels and restaurants needed food to serve and visitors were in need of food to eat!

Griffith died in 1885. He led a life of love and devastation, but didn't let his sorrows overcome him, and established a successful business in the new development of the town. This venture was profitable enough to continue to provide for his family after he had gone. Owen carried on with the management of the grocery business. In 1897 Ann drew up her will, making provision for her family, and died in 1903, her death announced in the Family Notices section of *Llandudno Advertiser and List of Visitors* as *'October 3rd, at Gronant House, Llandudno, aged 85, Ann Owen, widow of the late Griffith Owen. Interred at St Tudno's Church, October 6th.'*[69] Today Gronant House is occupied by the business Babi Seren.

Thomas Jones

Some miners were born locally and lived their whole lives as residents of Llandudno, whereas others, like Thomas Jones, were only inhabitants of the town for a relatively short time, just as the work of mining brought them to the area it also took them away from it.

Thomas Jones was born in Penrhos on Anglesey in 1810, the son of Evan and his wife Elizabeth Jones. In 1832 he married Letitia Thomas. Unusually for this time, Thomas signed the parish register for his marriage himself, so he had obviously been educated to read and write, whereas more commonly what is seen is a simple 'X' in

69 *North Wales Chronicle* – Tuesday 06 August 1844

Pictured: (seated) Letitia and Benjamin William Jones. (standing) William Lester and Benjamin's niece Letitia Ann. Photo used with kind permission of Thomas Jones' direct descendant Mark Jones.

lieu of a signature, where a person left their mark, as Letitia did.

By the time the 1841 census was taken Thomas and his wife were living in Talar in St Asaph, and had had two children Ann and John. The census also shows that Thomas was a miner, an occupation that took him through various regions of North Wales, according to where work was available. By the time their seventh child was born in 1848 Thomas and Letitia had moved to Llandudno where again Thomas put his mining skills to use. In 1854 the pair had a son called Benjamin William, and this son would one day verbally relay his memories of his father and Victorian Llandudno to his daughter, Letitia Jones Boulton, who wrote them all down to preserve for future generations. When Benjamin made these recollections, Llandudno was distant in both memory and geography, by then he lived in Utah, however the detail he provided is indicative of the fond memories he had of the village. The following is an excerpt from these recollections:

'*I was born on September 12, 1854 in Llandidno Carvinshire,* [sic] *North Wales, in a tall rock house with a wall around it. As near as I can remember, we lived there until I was quite a big boy.*

I can remember a little wagon that my father bought me. I also remember an apple tree with apples on it which grew in the yard. Guess it was the pretty red apples which make me remember this.

My father's house was built of stone at the base of the Great Horn [sic] *Mountain. The beach circled in a horseshoe shape around the mountain with lots of mulberry bushes growing near it. You could look along the shore from our house for five miles. There was a hotel built here which helped to make this mountain and seashore a most beautiful sight to see*'.

These recollections were dictated by Benjamin to his daughter, which might explain 'Orme' being misheard for '*Horn*'. In his recollections Benjamin talks of how his father, Thomas Jones, was a talented musician and inspired him in learning to play an instrument. We know from the parish register that Thomas could read and write, and this was something that he wanted to pass onto his son, clearly education was important to him, so he sent Benjamin to school.

The family did not settle in Llandudno, and by the time of the 1861 census had moved to Bwlch Gwyn where Thomas continued to work as a miner. Though he only lived in Llandudno for just over a decade, it was long enough for Thomas to be remembered as a member of the community, mentioned some years later in Rowlands' *Adgofion am Landudno*. Rowlands remembers Thomas Jones as someone who '*could tell all there was to know about Joseph Smith, his revelations, his miracles and the supreme importance of sacrificing all in order to emigrate to Salt Lake City.*' It is unclear whether Thomas and his family were converted to Mormonism after the religious movement arrived in Llandudno, or whether Thomas was one of the missionaries that brought the faith to the area.

It is clear that charity was a pillar of Thomas' character, for he and Letitia adopted a child, William Lester, who was born in Liverpool in 1854, while the family were living in Llandudno. A very selfless act given the stretch on resources another child would have added to their already large family. William Lester was a foundling, left on a doorstep but the Jones family, the generous people they were, raised him and he became one of their children.

After finishing his shift mining on 24th June 1867, Thomas started to feel ill, not making it home from the local shop and as he walked through a field he fell to the ground, in pain and was found by a neighbour who sought help. The next day he died, but before he passed he asked Benjamin to care for his mother.

Making the voyage ahead of him, Benjamin's siblings set out for America and in time Benjamin and Letitia followed them to Utah. In moving to the United States with Letitia, Benjamin was holding firm to the promise that he had made to his father before he died and realised the dreams that Thomas had had for his family to find their place in Salt Lake City.

The Heart of The Community

These men were essential to the functioning of the town and its physical construction and maintenance. Although all of those included in this book can easily qualify to be included in this chapter, beyond their occupations as miners these individuals performed roles that were essential to the geographical growth and tourism of the town and as such put them at the centre of their community.

In the foreground, the headstone of William Brookes and several other of his family members, in St Tudno's Churchyard.

William Brookes

Although they shared a name, this miner is not related to the William Brookes who died in an accident in the mines in 1847.

In '*Adgofion am Landudno*' Thomas Rowlands said '*There is no one today who knows more of the history of Llandudno and the mines than Mr. William Brookes... if he undertook to record his memories they would be an invaluable record for future generations*'. Unfortunately I am unaware of any such memoir left by William Brookes.

Born in 1816 William was the eldest son of George and Anne of Llwyn Helyg, Llandudno. Being born into a family where his father was a mine manager it is unsurprising that William also followed his father into a career in copper mining. On the 1841 census he is listed as a miner, as well as on the 1851 and 1871 censuses too. By 1841 the family had also relocated to The Victoria, an inn and said to be the largest house in Llandudno at that time. This was the home where William would live out the rest of his life.

He had a change of career in 1861 where he is listed as '*Inspector of Nuisances*'. This position in the town meant that it was William's job to monitor and inspect public health and sanitation, the safety of buildings as well as a broad scope of other environmental tasks, the job being a very early forerunner for Environmental Health. William would have seen some unpleasant sights in the role, but the fact that he held it also suggests his esteem in the town, as the health and safety of its inhabitants was entrusted to him.

On the 1881 census William is cited as being a Fire Clay Works Manager and by 1891 the last of the Llandudno mines had closed, though William is still recorded on that year's census as being a copper miner, perhaps reflecting how he identified himself.

Although it seems that William left no memoirs of his own, he is remembered in those of others, in Thomas Rowlands' as mentioned on previous page, and also by John Williams. In 1911 Williams recalled that Brookes worked at Tŷ Gwyn Mine.

William Brookes died aged 80 in June of 1896 and was buried in St Tudno's Churchyard. *Llandudno Advertiser and List of Visitors stated how he 'was highly respected by all who knew him...held in great esteem by old and young...a good old fashioned Welshman'.*[70]

John Edwards

Born in 1786, John would go onto live a very long life and have a very large family. During his life he saw the copper mines of Llandudno go from being some of the most industrious in the country to their twilight period and closure.

A native of Amlwch his parents were Samuel and Mary, but by 1815 he had moved to Llandudno and met the woman who would become his wife, Sarah Jones. On the 1841 and 1851 censuses John is

70 *Llandudno Advertiser and List of Visitors* – 18th June 1896

listed as working as a miner, but by the time the 1861 census was taken he had changed professions, reflective of the changing economic climate of Llandudno at that time, and was working as a cab driver. In this capacity he collected passengers from Conwy to bring them to Llandudno, a key role in the town's burgeoning tourism industry. It seems that he had not turned his back entirely on mining though, on the 1871 census he is documented as a miner once more, before enjoying a well-earned retirement in the decade following, as in 1881 'Old Age' is officially his occupation!

Between at least 1851 and his death he lived at Tan Rallt, surrounded by the company of other long-established members of the local mining community, his neighbours being families such as the Rawlings, many of whom attended his funeral following his death in June of 1884. His obituary in *The North Wales Chronicle* describes him fondly as being '*a familiar face in the town with his stick and umbrella*'[71] right up until his death.

Thomas Rowlands recalled John's funeral as '*one of the strangest ever seen in the place because of the number of his own family who attended*'. Rowlands is referring to the large amount of descendants John lived to see born within his lifetime. A funeral of this magnitude was one to be remembered in Llandudno, conveying the amount of people that loved and respected John. At the time of his death he left behind a legacy of sixty-two great grandchildren, meaning there are many living in Llandudno today and far beyond that can call John their ancestor.

Enoch and Ellen Hughes

Another '*excellent character*' of Llandudno as described by Thomas Rowlands was Enoch Hughes. Born in Anglesey in 1801 by the time of the 1841 census he was living in a house owned by George Brookes (agent of Tŷ Gwyn mine) and working in Llandudno as a copper miner.

By the late 1850s Enoch, his wife Ellen and their family had moved to Bedford House, a property that the Hughes family would run as a lodging house and although Enoch was still labouring away in the mines he was also the manager of this business.[72]

---

71 *North Wales Chronicle* – Saturday June 28th 1884.

72 *The North Wales Chronicle and Advertiser for the Principality* – 15th August 1857

Ellen is listed as being the Lodging Housekeeper assisted by her two daughters, Mary and Hannah. The household would have been a very lively one, as the List of Visitors published in local newspapers reflects, with people staying with them from various different towns and cities in England.

However, in 15th August 1857 edition of *The North Wales Chronicle and Advertiser for the Principality* Bedford House is without any listed visitors. There was nonc of thc usual hubbub taking place in the house that week as only a few days before, on the 9th August a tragedy had befallen the Hughes family, Enoch and Ellen had lost their son Benjamin. The words etched onto his headstone in Welsh speak of their love and mourning for the loss of their son when he was twenty-eight, at an age when he would have been beginning to make his mark on the world. In the years before Benjamin died he had been working as a joiner, having started out in his teenage ycars like many others, as an agricultural labourer.

Copper Ddu Shaft (aka Vivian's Shaft) in the foreground and Pyllau Shaft (painted white), the site of Old Mine. Date unknown.

At this time Bedford House was in grave mourning but a couple of weeks later Enoch and Ellen had to dig deep emotionally, find the strength to continue, with some sort of normality resuming by the end of August, as visitors are once again listed as staying at the premises.

Working as a copper miner and managing a lodging house must have been extremely hard work and meant Enoch had to juggle different aspects of his professional life, but he also found time to make clogs for the miners in what little spare time he had. As a miner himself he would have known the importance of having good and reliable footwear when working in the belly of the Orme!

Enoch died at his home on Church Walks on 27th February 1870 and was buried on 3rd March, in the same plot as his son Benjamin lay in St Tudno's Churchyard. The sole executor of his will was his wife, he left property valued at under a hundred pounds, which does not sound a lot from the perspective of the twenty-first century, but would have been a considerable amount in the nineteenth. Ellen moved in with her daughter Mary and her family after Enoch's death, before she died in 1874. She was buried alongside her husband and son.

Joseph Hughes

Born in Llandudno to Joseph Hughes and Ann (nee Edwards), like many other children in the town, Joseph Hughes was washing copper ore before he was nine years old. Apparently very good at it, he was sent to Llansannan when he was thirteen to teach the children of that village the skill. At fourteen, though still only very young, he obviously had ambitions, and with the money he had saved from his work, spent it wisely and went to Liverpool to receive an education, having saved a total of £7. When the money from his savings had run out, he returned to Llandudno and threw himself into his mining career.

In 1846 he became a contractor in the construction of the stone pillars of the Conwy Bridge, along with his father. An astute individual, Joseph continued to save his earnings. During the time that Llandudno was developing itself as a seaside resort his mining career would take him from North Wales, to Ireland, where he was employed in a management role and he remained there for around three years. While Joseph was in Ireland his father constructed the Mereville and the Belmont, to fund this building

Joseph Hughes as pictured in Papur Pawb, 2nd April 1902

enterprise to his parents Joseph forwarded all his savings.

On his return from Ireland Joseph went into partnership with his brother John, and the pair opened a builder's store and with people in their employment, began construction on a large scale. In 1860 he married Mary Anne Owen and the couple went on to have a large family. On the 1861 census Joseph is listed as a Stone Mason employing 5 Stone Masons and a further 6 labourers. On the 1871 Census he is a master builder and living with his family in the Washington Hotel on East Parade, where now stands Dylan's Restaurant (the original Washington Hotel was demolished in 1925).

Joseph was a man of religion and a deacon in the Baptist cause, throughout his life maintaining his faith, and a keen advocate of temperance. In later life he became a councillor for the town. Contemporary accounts note how he was a leading contributor to the town's growth. In 1902 *Papur Pawb* wrote a feature on Joseph going all the way back to his earliest memories. In that article it is stated that from a very early age Joseph had been raised in a religious environment, his dad having been baptised in the sea at Llandudno.

In his eighties Joseph was working as a teacher in the town's Sunday School, inspiring another generation that would ultimately come to shape Llandudno in the first part of the twentieth century.

In February of 1904 at the age of eighty-two Joseph died suddenly, due to heart failure. The *Carnarvon and Denbigh Herald* described him as '*genial in disposition, and straightforward in all his dealings*', his loss felt not just by his family and friends, but the whole community whom he had served well. I believe *The Llandudno Advertiser* best describes the contributions he had made to the town when they said '*few single individuals did more for Llandudno than Mr Joseph Hughes*'.

Dafydd / David Jones

As I have mentioned already, not all of those that played a significant part in Llandudno's mining industry were miners, and this applies to David Jones, for he was not a miner at all, but a farmer. So, how has a nineteenth century Llandudno dairy farmer come to be included in a book about the town's copper mining past?

David Jones was born in Llandudno in 1799, son of Hugh and Elizabeth Jones and in 1833 he married Margaret Hughes in her hometown of Amlwch. Once married Margaret came to live with her husband at Tŷ Draw, a farm once located close to where the Loretto Convent on Abbey Road stands today. The pair had children and became core members of the mining village community, they were later described as having been one of Llandudno's original families.

At Tŷ Draw David had several powerful horses stabled for the purposes of his work with Old Mine. These horses would be used to take supplies up Great Orme to Old Mine, once there what the horses had pulled up would be unloaded, the empty cart and a sledge attached behind would be reloaded with approximately half a ton of copper ore. Half a ton is a great amount of weight to pull down the steep descent of Great Orme on wheels and potentially very dangerous. To prevent the cart from getting carried away by the forces of gravity and causing an accident, the attached sledge behind acted as a brake, the friction of the ore's weight keeping it firmly grounded and ensuring a safe transportation. Once safely down the Great Orme David would take the ore to the washing floors, for preparation and loading onto one of the beached vessels for transportation to Amlwch.

David was an intrinsic and essential part of the mining operations in

A beached sailing vessel on Llandudno's North Shore, waiting to be loaded with copper ore, by one such as David Jones.
Image with thanks to Don Smith

Llandudno. He played the vital role between miner and ore dresser, for the ore could only bring profit if it was hauled down the Orme and sold. This is to say nothing of his role in the community that Thomas Rowlands referred to when he said '*David and Margaret Jones were honest to the T. The very impersonation of kindness and benevolence, and for that reason they "had the poor always with them." They supplied a great part of the village with sweet milk, butter milk, butter, and any other farm produce, while their splendid teams and men were always ready when their assistance was required by the poor miners.*' (Llandudno Advertiser)[73]. David was routinely a source of support for the miners, both in a logistical sense and in keeping up their morale. It was said that people could go to him for help, and he would always offer his assistance, even if it meant putting himself out of pocket. With the supplying of good food and good counsel, David and his wife Margaret made themselves important cogs in the success of Llandudno's copper mining enterprises.

Sometime between 1851 and 1861 the family vacated Tŷ Draw Farm and settled on Mostyn Street from where David worked exclusively as a carter. In 1866 Margaret died leaving David a widower. Years later Rowlands remembered her as '*never a more honest person than Margaret Jones and she would sooner have cast all her belongings into the sea than to engage in dishonest trading*'. Following Margaret's death David moved in with his sister and her family and died in 1878. By 1892 Tŷ Draw was in ruins, but the kindness and generosity of its former inhabitants was long remembered.

Joseph Tamblyn

Joseph Tamblyn (sometimes spelled 'Tamblin' or 'Tambling') was the son of a mine agent. Joseph had been born in Cornwall and moved to Flintshire when he was still a boy, and by the time he arrived in Llandudno in 1834 he was already a married man, he had married Mary Jones in the first half of that decade. Joseph found work as a pitman engineer for Old Mine, and of all those working at the mine at that time who were in receipt of a weekly wage, he was the highest earner. Evidently skilled in his trade, perhaps it is no coincidence that he commenced his appointment at Old Mine the same year that work began on constructing the Pen Morfa Adit.

No doubt though that Joseph Tamblyn's biggest impact on Llandudno was his advocacy for the Wesleyan cause, establishment of a Methodist Society and determination to build a chapel of worship for that faith. When he first arrived in Llandudno there was no Methodist Society in the town, so Joseph invited a preacher named John Owen from Gyffin to conduct services at his house at Tŷ

73 *Llandudno Advertiser and List of Visitors* – 18th June 1896

The property that once was Caersalem Chapel. The plaque on where once was the door commemorates Australian Prime Minister William Morris Hughes who was educated in the building following its use as a place of worship.

Coch Bach. Eventually through Joseph's determination and dedication to his faith Caersalem Chapel was constructed on Cwlach Street and opened in March of 1837. As he had been a champion for its construction naturally Joseph became a trustee for the chapel before he eventually left Llandudno. In the 1861 publication *Llandudno Its History and Natural History* Richard Parry describes this chapel as being '*neat and commodious*'.

In 1875 Caersalem would cease to function as a place of worship, but by that time Joseph Tamblyn had long since left the town and had ceased to work in the mining industry, returning to Flintshire and becoming a grocer. Some years after Tamblyn had left Llandudno Thomas Rowlands remembered Joseph and his wife in his recollections of Old Llandudno when he said '*Joseph and Mary Tamblin could provide details of the founding of the Wesleyan Cause here*'.

Though Caersalem no longer operated as a chapel it remained a very useful building, becoming a school where many, including William Morris Hughes who would go onto become Prime Minister of Australia, would be educated. This building still stands today as a private residence, acting as tangible evidence of Joseph's impact on the town and his energising of Wesleyan Methodism in Llandudno.

Joseph died in 1897 in Prestatyn and was buried in St Michael's churchyard in Caerwys, Flintshire. On recording his passing local publication *Denbighshire Free Press* described him as having been a '*gentleman*' whose funeral was well attended by a large number of mourners.

The Victoria Tram Station on Church Walks, where once stood The Victoria Inn, at one time the largest house in Llandudno.

The Captains and Agents

Many of the Llandudno agents and captains hailed originally from Cornwall, with their work bringing them north to the shores of Llandudno. The work of a captain was not an easy one, the role was one that had to act as mediator between mine owner and miners and this could sometimes put them in an unenviable position. Here are just some of the men that had to navigate the professional line between employee and employer.

Tŷ Gwyn Mine

George Brookes

In 1788 George was born in Llanasa, the son of William and Ann Brookes. He married his wife Ann and settled in Llandudno. By the time their first child was born George was working as a Llandudno copper miner and the family were living at Llwyn Helyg, on Great Orme but by 1839 had moved to Victoria Inn. Over the years George and Ann would have a large family of eleven children.

As George started his career as a miner and rose through the ranks to become an agent, he was well qualified for the go-between role that was Mine Agent, a role that involved liaising between miners and mine owners and since he's described as having been '*well liked*' in the town it seems he fulfilled this position admirably. He had worked at Old Mine before becoming Tŷ Gwyn Mine's agent, so had a broad practical knowledge of the various different workings in the Orme.

Tŷ Gwyn Mine closed in 1853 following a flood of water into the mine's workings so unexpectedly it was reported that the miners had to flee and leave their tools behind them, never to be retrieved again. For George he had his business as an innkeeper at The Victoria to provide him with an income, and he owned a few cottages on Cwlach Road too. So although the flooding happened in a flash, he was well prepared to adapt and survive in the town's tourism economy once the mining enterprise he was involved in ceased business.

He died on 11th October 1858 at the age

of seventy and was buried in St Tudno's Churchyard. Eventually his son George in 1876, and wife Ann in 1880, would be buried alongside him. However his legacy continued to live on in archaeology, George had been respectful and conscious of the need to preserve the ancient artefacts found in the mine. In 1859 a stone tool that he had discovered in the mine and donated to Warrington Museum was reported on in *The Warrington Standard and Lancashire and Cheshire Advertiser* following the find's examination by the British Archaeological Association.

The Great Orme Tramway's Victoria Station on Church Walks is the site of where once stood the Victoria Inn, and the station takes its name from the Brookes family home, so George and his family's presence in the town is remembered to this day and is seen by the many thousands of passengers that pass through this station every year.

In the foreground, the final resting place of Old Mine agent Jonathan Rawling.

Old Mine

Jonathan Rawling

Jonathan Rawling was born in the village of Perranarworthal in Cornwall in the winter of 1783 to his parents Jonathan and

Ann. In June of 1820 he had relocated to Liverpool where he married his wife, Jane Owens. Jane was cited on the marriage banns as being of Caernarfon but Jonathan as being of Liverpool St Peter. It is unclear how the pair met, whether it was in Wales or England. Perhaps Jonathan had visited the Llandudno mines before commencing work in the town and during the visit to the area met the woman that would become his wife? By 1829 the pair were living in Llandudno where their son Thomas was born.

Jonathan was employed by the Worthington brothers as the mine agent of Old Mine and resided in the house named Tŷ Glas on Church Walks which would continue to be the home of the agents of Old Mine thereafter.

Jonathan died on 8th December of 1836, at the age of 55. His headstone bears the following inscription:

'Here lieth the Body of Jonathan Rawling late Agent to the old Mine Company at this place who departed this life on the 8th Dec 1836 Aged 55

This stone was placed as a token of respect by his late employers'.

That his employers laid the headstone speaks loudly of the high regard they and the Llandudno community had for Jonathan.

Ann outlived her husband by over thirty years, reaching the age of seventy-nine, passing away in the August of 1870. She was buried in the same grave as her husband. Today many of Llandudno's residents can trace their lineage back to Jonathan and Ann.

John Williams

Those who are already familiar with the story of Llandudno's origins as a seaside resort will have heard of John Williams before. For those that have not, the romantic story of how he and Lord Mostyn met with a visitor to the town from Liverpool named Owen Williams and discussed the prospects of turning the small mining village into a bathing resort is often trotted out to tourists visiting the area. This story does not do justice to the extent of work that John Williams put into Llandudno.

Born in 1811 in Llanbeblig as a young man he was employed in assisting his uncle in his work. John's uncle was the agent of the Mostyn family, and in shadowing his uncle in his duties this was an apprenticeship that John obviously exceeded in, as in 1827 he took over from his uncle in the role and became Lord Mostyn's agent himself. He married Jane Evans in Llanrhos in 1836 and by 1841 he and his family are living at Bryn y Bia, Bodafon, Llandudno. It was during the 1840s that John Williams was the agent of both Old and Tŷ Gwyn mines. In 1843 it was advertised in the *Chester Courant* that shares in Tŷ Gwyn Mine were to be sold at the end of December, and that enquiries regarding the sale should be directed to John Williams of Bodafon. Only three years later, in 1846, John would find himself playing an important role in the sale of another Llandudno mine, this time Old Mine, drawing up a thorough report of the business, its facilities, infrastructure and inventory, which no doubt was invaluable to the new owners of the business and today remains an important document for studying the history of the site. However, John's most memorable work that decade would come from a meeting he had between Lord Mostyn and Owen Williams, where the Llandudno we know today had its foundations laid and the town would never be the same again.

The story of John Williams' involvement in the origins of Llandudno has gone on to live in the collective memory of the town's residents because it has all the hallmarks of being the stuff of legend. In 1846 a man named Owen Williams had accompanied a friend to Llandudno, the latter had some business to conduct at one of the mines. Upon getting off the boat Owen was awestruck by the beauty of the bay and voiced his opinion that Llandudno would make a fantastic bathing resort. Some hours later, over a meal in the Kings Head, Owen and his friend would return to this topic. Owen Williams recalled the following some years after; '*Mr. Mostyn informed me that his agent (the late Mr. John Williams of Bodafon) who was present at the dinner had mentioned to him the suggestion I had made...his agent and myself took possession of a very primitive sort of bathing box on the edge of the shore... In that box was our first meeting and conversation*'[74]. John was evidently a shrewd man of business, had heard Owen discussing his idea in the pub and wasted

74 *Llandudno and The Mostyn Influence*, F. Ron Williams.

Early image of Llandudno as a booming seaside resort, the crowd showing how popular Llandudno had become. Somewhere in the distance is the location of the hut where John Williams, Owen Williams and Lord Mostyn met.

no time in relaying this idea to the Mostyns, and set up the meeting that would take place 'bathing box' on North Shore. In the tale of Llandudno's origins and how it is often told to visitors, this is where generally the story leaves off, with John having got the ball rolling, and the three meeting. However for John the work had only just begun.

In the years that followed John Williams was at the heart of this transformation from mining village to seaside resort, purpose built for leisure. It could be argued that he was the original tourist board for the town, getting Llandudno the media exposure it needed to attract visitors, having journals published in England, these articles spoke of the town's beauty and the advantages it had for benefiting one's health. Beyond his direct involvement in the development of the town he was also a clerk to the Llandudno Improvement Commissioners, a guardian of the poor and a secretary of various organisations including the Llandudno Gas and Water Company to name but only a few of the roles he held.

I do not have enough space here to sufficiently explore the extent of the huge impact that John Williams had on Llandudno in growing it into the town we recognise today, however I feel that this impact is best summarised by *The North Wales Chronicle* on reporting his death in 1876 when they said that Llandudno is '*a noble and copious monument of his success*'.

John was laid to rest in St Hilary's Churchyard in the same grave as two of his sons that had predeceased him. His funeral was on Saturday 17th June 1876 and involved a large procession of more than sixty carriages and hundreds of people following on foot, indicative of the amount of lives that John had touched and the respect that not just Llandudno residents had for him, but those of the wider area and beyond. His headstone reads 'they rest from their labours and their works do follow them' and what a lot of work John Williams put into Llandudno! Work that we are still benefiting from almost a hundred and fifty years after his death.

William Vivian

William Vivian is one of the more commonly known mining Captains, and this is possibly due to Vivian's Shaft, one of the workings of Old Mine and now part of the Great Orme Mines visitor attraction complex. However, the shaft was not named after the Cornish mine captain, but instead had its moniker in the decades before Vivian came to Llandudno. So when, how and why did William Vivian come to be in Llandudno, and if not the mining shaft, does any trace of his time in the town exist today?

Born in Redruth, Cornwall, William Vivian was appointed Captain of Old Mine in 1853 when John Taylor and Sons purchased the mine and setup The

William Vivian in his fifties.

Llandudno Company. Immediately that he commenced work in his new role he had challenges on his hands. By the time John Taylor and Sons took over the site it had fallen into disrepair. In 1853 Vivian wrote that he had '*found the mine entirely out of order*' and had to begin on rectifying this situation before any attempt at mining could be made. Before Vivian could make ingress on the necessary improvements though, there was industrial action.

Many of the Llandudno miners had other jobs beyond mining, and working as a miner was supplemented by work as a fisherman, farmer and other occupations, so they mined in six hour shifts, which allowed them time to fulfil their other commitments. However, when John Taylor and Sons took over the mine they wanted more productivity from the staff than a mining shift of six hours afforded and demanded that the miners work eight hour days. The workers of Old Mine went on strike, making a stand for the preservation of the conditions they had always had. The miners of Old Mine remained on strike most of the year and in the meantime the poor state of the site continued to decay.

For Vivian as the go-between from miner to mine owner, he was in a difficult position, told by the company to demand eight hours of work from his men. The poor condition of the site along with the industrial action must have made making the site productive again feel to Vivian like an impossible task. To his great credit though, despite the odds, he did turn it around into productivity. In December of 1853 the *Daily News* published that William

Vivian reported that he had '110 hands at work' at Old Mine.

1853 was certainly a busy year in William Vivian's life, new job, new home and he had also married, a woman named Jane Mitchell. Whilst living in Llandudno the pair would have several children, born at Tŷ Glas. For a while William enjoyed success and happiness in both his professional and personal life.

Vivian conducted scientific studies of the Orme and in 1858 found '*microscopic arborescent crystallisation*'[75] of native copper (copper that occurs in the ground naturally and has not gone through the process of smelting) in brown limestone on Great Orme. On this discovery he wrote an essay that was published in the Journal for the Geological Society and this was regarded with '*high interest*'[76] by his contemporaries. What he had discovered at Old Mine made the site something of a place of curiosity to geologists and '*scientific tourists*'[77] with a member of Worcester Natural History Field Club visiting him at the mine in the August of that year.

However, the professional and scientific success he enjoyed in the summer of 1858 was to be overshadowed that autumn as a dark cloud was about to descend upon the Vivian family. This was the mid-nineteenth century and no life was without sorrow, and that October William and Jane lost their son John at just three years old.

Pushing through his grief and continuing his work, in 1860 Vivian gave a talk in Llandudno on the geological wonders of Great Orme. That evening the audience was apparently very large, which speaks of the town's residents' regard for Vivian's subject knowledge as well as their appetite for learning.

William's biggest impact upon the town was arguably his contributions to the Methodist cause. Llandudno was growing as a tourist resort and it was important for many visitors that they should have access to English language worship while they stayed in the town, and so as a local preacher Captain William Vivian led these English services. Eventually a need for a

75 *The Mining Journal* – 26th June 1858.
76 *North Wales Chronicle* – Saturday 28 August 1858
77 *North Wales Chronicle* – Saturday 28 August 1858

Methodist Church to be built was raised and a meeting at Tŷ Glas, Vivian's home, was held for beginning the arrangements and plans for setting this in motion. Although it was not until some years after Vivian had left Llandudno that St John's Church was built, he had been part of those early talks and proposals for the building of a centre of worship that still stands and remains in use today.

Vivian continued to have a successful career after leaving Llandudno and died in 1879, upon his death was described as having been an '*excellent agent...with utmost scrupulous truth and fidelity*'.[78]

78 *West Briton and Cornwall Advertiser* – Thursday 01 May 1879

Bibliography

LLANDUDNO CONFERENCE 1939
The Educational Publishing Company
Cardiff and Wrexham.
1939.

THOMAS KENDRICK LLANDUDNO'S CAVE MAN
Dr. Cleanth Jones.
Gwasg Helygain.
2013.

PAUPERS, BASTARDS AND LUNATICS
Christopher Draper.
Gwasg Carreg Gwalch.
2005.
ISBN 978-0-86381-879-0

LLANDUDNO LIFEBOATS
Nicholas Leech.
Foxglove Publishing.
2019.
ISBN 9781909540125

A TOILSOME TASK OF INDUSTRY
J. Richard Williams.
Gwasg Carreg Gwalch.
2013.
ISBN 978-1-8427-403-0

LLANDUDNO BEFORE THE HOTELS
Christopher Draper.
Gwasg Carreg Gwalch.
2007
ISBN 978-1-84524-095-0

MYNYDD PARYS
Owen Griffith (translated in 2006 by Tom Parry)
Coastline Publications
2008

GREAT ORME MINES
C. J. Williams.
The Northern Mine Research Society
1995
ISBN 0 901450 43 X

THE GREAT ORME COPPER MINES
Don Smith.
Creuddyn Publications
1991
ISBN 0 9514051 01

THE HISTORY OF THE LLANDUDNO BAPTISTS
Trustees of the Tabernacl.
1969 – 1972

THE CROSSING OF THE CONWY
Michael Senior.
Gwasg Carreg Gwalch
2009
ISBN 978-1-84524-066-0

SHIPWRECKS OF NORTH WALES
Ivor Wynne Jones.
Landmark Collector's Library
2001
ISBN 9 781843 060055

LLANDUDNO AND THE MOSTYN INFLUENCE
F. Ron Williams.
T. Davies & Son
1996
ISBN 9 781898 202066

LLANDUDNO: ITS HISTORY AND NATURAL HISTORY
Richard Parry.
HardPress
2019
ISBN 9 780461 435177

LLANDUDNO A HISTORY AND CELEBRATION
Derek Roberts.
Frith Book Company
2004
ISBN 978-1904938361

BRITISH MINING No. 50 MEMOIRS 1994 – THE LIFE AND ESSAYS OF WILLIAM VIVIAN, CORNISH MINING ENGINEER, 1817 – 1879.
Don Smith.
Northern Mine Research Society
1994
ISSN 03082199

SO GREAT A CLOUD
Ron Jones.
St John's Methodist Church, Llandudno
2020.

A colourised photo of the remains of one of the Old Mine buildings, 1954, D. Geriant Griffith 'A Study of the Economic Development of the Lower Conwy Valley and Creuddyn Peninsula. Image with thanks to Conwy Archives, Conwy County Borough Council.

Acknowledgements

Many thanks to the following people and organisations that have supported me in this publication:

The Great Orme Mines team particularly Nick Jowett, Andy Lewis, Edric Roberts, Tony Hammond and Harriet White.

Tom Parry for his wealth of information provided so kindly.

Adrian Hughes of The Home Front Museum.

Don Smith.

The staff of Conwy Archives.

David Wrennall and others of The Great Orme Exploration Society.

The Llandudno Historical Society for Adrian Hughes' letter.

The relatives and descendants of those I've written about, such relatives include: Jason Edwards, Allan Stevenson, Bethan Jones, Iona Goldsmith, Mark and Cheryl Jones, David Collins, Norman Rogers-Jones, Hannah Miles and James Hobson.

Notes on the Copyrights

Introduction

Circa 1900 postcard of Maes y Facrell, copyrights unknown. Widely published.

Chroniclers and Collectors

Image of Thomas Kendrick from Thomas Kendrick Library.

Image of Thomas Rowlands from Conwy Archive Conwy County Borough Council (reference CP163/11/96).

Image of John Williams' former home, 2 Cromlech Road, with kind permission of Rebecca Devany.

Heroes and Heroism

Image of Samuel Edwards' medal and certificate with permission from his direct descendant Jason Edwards.

Image of Hugh Jones from Conwy Archive, Conwy County Borough Council, (reference CP251/9).

Image of Y Fach (Happy Valley) author's own.

Women of the Copper Mines

Image of Elizabeth Lester's headstone in St Tudno's churchyard author's own.

Image of Maes y Facrell Nature Reserve author's own.

Image of Pen y Buarth, Great Orme from Conwy Archive, Conwy County Borough Council (reference CP395/3/820).

Image of Old Mine, copyright unknown. Widely published.

Tragedies and Survivors

Image of William Brookes' headstone, author's own.

Image of Bathing machines at North Shore, Llandudno, c. 1880; National Media Museum Collection, WikiMedia Commons.

Image of John and Jane Smith's graves in St George's Churchyard, author's own.

Image of Conwy Hospital, the old workhome; Chris Draper from his book *Pauper, Bastards and Lunatics*).

Image of John Griffith from Conwy Archive, Conwy County Borough Council (reference CP251/90)

Image of Penmeanbach Railway Tunnel from Conwy Archive, Conwy County Borough Council (reference CP465/2/5).

Image of Conwy Tubular Bridge; Picken, Thomas, d. 1891, lithographer through Creative Commons)

Image of Thomas Jones' headstone, author's own.

Image of Copper Ddu (Vivian's) Shaft, author's own.

Image of the ciffs of Great Orme, author's own.

The Innovators and The Esteemed

Image of the area surrounding Bishops Quarry Road prior to the building of the upper section of the tram track donated to author by Tom Parry.

Image of Catherine Hughes' headstone author's own.

Images of aerial view of Bryniau Poethion with thanks to Great Orme Mines.

Image of Richard Hughes from Conwy Archive, CCBC (reference CP137/1)

Image of the miner's clog obtained from Don Smith.

Image of Edward Owens with permission from his direct descendant Norman Rogers-Jones.

Image of Llwyn Helyg, Pen y Gwaith, author's own.

Image of St George's Church author's own.

The Almost, But Should Never Be, Forgotten

Image of Thomas Lloyd's headstone author's own.

Image of Felclia Simpson's 1853 watercolour – taken from a copy(?) held at Great Orme Mines.

Image of Barbara Powell standing outside her home with others by kind permission of David Collins.

Image of Marg. Thomas' headstone author's own.

Image of West Shore Boating Pond author's own.

Image of Madoc Street 1920s from Conwy Archive, CCBC (reference unknown – from a bundle possibly CP range).

Image of Benjamin William Jones and family with kind permission of Mark W. Jones.

The Heat of the Community

Image of William Brookes' grave author's own.

Image of the site of Old Mine (date unknown, possibly 1900 – 1920) part of author purchased.

Image of Joseph Hughes from *Papur Pawb* 5th April 1902, No. 479, pg 6, col 1 The National Library of Wales.

Image of beached sailing vessel on Llandudno's North Shore, waiting to be loaded with copper ore, by one such as David Jones. With thanks to Don Smith.

Image of the property on Cwlach Street that once was Caersalem Chapel, author's own.

The Captains and The Agents

Image of Victoria tram station author's own.

Image of Jonathan Rawling's grave author's own.

Image of Llandudno nineteenth century beach scene from Tom Parry's collection.

Image of William Vivian obtained from Don Smith (used in his 1994 essay with permission from the Vivian descendants).

Acknowledgements

Image of the area of Old Mine, showing old mine building, from D. Geriant Griffith's 1954 '*A Study of the Economic Development of the Lower Conwy Valley and Creuddyn Peninsula*', now in Conwy Archives, Conwy County Borough Council.